As one of the world's longest establish[ed]
and best-known travel bran[ds]
Thomas Cook are the experts in tra[vel]

For more than 135 years [our]
guidebooks have unlocked the se[crets]
of destinations around the w[orld]
sharing with travellers a wea[lth of]
experience and a passion for travel.

**Rely on Thomas Cook as your
travelling companion on your next trip
and benefit from our unique heritage.**

Thomas Cook **traveller** guides

VANCOUVER &
BRITISH COLUMBIA
Carol Baker

Your travelling companion since 1873

Written by Carol Baker, updated by Maxine Cass
Original photography by Helena Zukowski

Published by Thomas Cook Publishing
A division of Thomas Cook Tour Operations Limited
Company registration no. 3772199 England
The Thomas Cook Business Park, 9 Coningsby Road,
Peterborough PE3 8SB, United Kingdom
Email: books@thomascook.com, Tel: + 44 (0) 1733 416477
www.thomascookpublishing.com

Produced by Cambridge Publishing Management Limited
Burr Elm Court, Main Street, Caldecote CB23 7NU
www.cambridgepm.co.uk

ISBN: 978-1-84848-326-2

© 2002, 2006, 2008 Thomas Cook Publishing
This fourth edition © 2010
Text © Thomas Cook Publishing
Maps © Thomas Cook Publishing

Series Editor: Karen Beaulah
Production/DTP: Steven Collins

Printed and bound in Spain by GraphyCems

Cover photography: © Stefan Damm/SIME-4Corners Images

Contents

Background 4–15
Introduction 4
Land and people 6
History 10
Politics 13
Culture and events 14

First steps 16–21
Impressions 16

Destination guide 22–125
Vancouver 22
Vancouver environs 78
Vancouver's islands 100

Getting away from it all 126–39

Directory 140–89
Shopping 140
Entertainment 148
Children 154
Sport and leisure 156
Food and drink 164
Accommodation 172
Practical guide 176

Index 190–91

Maps
BC within Canada 7
British Columbia 21
Downtown Vancouver 23
Chinatown walk 31
Gastown walk 35
Art in public places walk 41
Pacific Spirit Park walk 46
Granville Island walk 57
The sea wall by bike 69
Boat ride on a bus tour 75
Vancouver environs 79
Bowen Island walk 97
Vancouver's islands 104
Victoria 106
Sunshine Circle tour 125

Features
The charm of Vancouver beaches 26
Chinese Canadians 32
The BC art scene 42
On the totem trail 50
Stanley Park attractions 66
Harbour life 72
Unknown Vancouver 76
Animal kingdom 86
Flowers in season 94
BC's birdlife 108
BC's lumber industry 120
The iron horse 134
Taking to the slopes 158

Walks and tours
Walk: Chinatown 30
Walk: Gastown 34
Tour: Vancouver Trolley 36
Walk: Art in public places 40
Walk: Pacific Spirit Park 46
Walk: Granville Island 56
By bike: The sea wall 68
Tour: Boat ride on a bus 74
Walk: Bowen Island 96
Tour: Sunshine Circle 124

Introduction

British Columbia, often referred to as BC, joined the Canadian Confederation in 1871. Its origins extend a long way back in time, to the creation of the majestic Coast Mountains, 130 million years ago. The north, with its extremes of temperature, is sparsely populated, while the sparkling waterfront urban centres of Vancouver and Victoria, where the climate is relatively temperate, indulge in year-round cultural offerings and a passion for enjoying the outdoors.

The first residents were Asian hunters and berry gatherers, who drifted south along the coast and into the interior around 6000 BC. The first visitor to arrive by sea was probably Hoei-Shin, a Chinese Buddhist priest who sailed across the Pacific in AD 499.

Although the Spanish explorer Balboa claimed the Pacific Ocean and all its shores for Spain in 1513, the Spaniards did not settle here until the late 18th century. They stayed only a few years, but left their names: Cardero, Valdez, Juan de Fuca, Bodega y Quadra and Malaspina. Explorations by adventurers such as Captain James Cook, Alexander Mackenzie, George Vancouver and Simon Fraser resulted in an influx of British settlers, and the area became a British colony in 1858.

Vancouver, Canada's Gateway to the Pacific, is a wonderfully cosmopolitan centre, often blending the best of both European and Asian ways of life, while at the same time encouraging a rebirth of BC's aboriginal First Nations cultures. Canada's third-largest city, with over two million residents, is home to half the province's population. It has looked westward across the Pacific to Asia for more than a century.

Jogging at Coal Harbour, Vancouver

BC's wild Pacific Coast

More than 430,000 Chinese Canadians now live in BC, most in Vancouver, and are a major and growing influence. Japanese and other Asians, along with Americans, Britons and Europeans, arrive as visitors on holidays, to marvel at the province's space, wilderness, native cultures and the slopes in Whistler, rated among the finest ski resorts in the world. As Canadian author Bruce Hutchison observed as long ago as 1953: '*The history of Canada for about three hundred years was a struggle to escape from the wilderness, and for the last half century has been a desperate attempt to escape into it.*'

Victoria, BC's sunny, laid-back capital city, displays its Victorian-era English underpinnings, especially the Parliament Buildings and nearby Fairmont Empress Hotel, which front the busy Inner Harbour.

When British Columbia, Vancouver and Whistler played host to the 2010 Winter Olympic and Paralympic Games, the secret was out: Canada's westernmost province has mountains galore, beaches, surf, forests, wildlife and wine country. Its urban reaches, from food, culture, parks and magnificent vistas, to traditions overlaid with forward-looking optimism, are equally ripe for exploration.

Land and people

The BC motto, Splendor Sine Occasu, *which means 'splendour undiminished', is almost an understatement. Canada's most westerly province comprises 944,735sq km (364,764sq miles) of remarkably diverse seascapes and landforms – solitary beaches, quiet coves, primeval rainforests, spectacular fjords, snow-capped ranges, tundra, alpine meadows, glacial lakes, pristine waterfalls, raging rivers, and gentle, thermal springs, verdant valleys, plains and deserts.*

Geological past

About 130 million years ago, a gigantic upheaval in the earth's crust created the majestic Coast Mountains, the beginning of present-day BC. Sixty-five million years ago, further movements brought forth the Rocky Mountains, and 40 million years later, Cascadia, the Atlantis of the Pacific, sank offshore, leaving Vancouver Island and Haida Gwaii (Queen Charlotte Islands) above sea level. A mere million years ago, most of BC was covered with a blanket of ice 2,500m (8,202ft) thick, which slowly began to recede 70,000 years later.

At one time, a thick layer of ice pressed down over the region; its retreat about 10,000 years ago left the vast and visually delightful panorama of mountains, canyons, fjords, rivers and swamps. Without the weight of the ice, the land lifted, and layers of marine shells have been found several hundred metres above sea level.

Fraser River delta land west of New Westminster developed after the ice retreated, and alluvial soils continue to create several metres of new real estate here every year.

In 1889, workers extending Granville Street unearthed ancient tools, weapons and ornaments in the Marpole Midden, the largest of its kind discovered in North America to that date. A similar midden in Stanley Park provided so

An early BC resident, Royal BC Museum, Victoria

many seashells, emptied and discarded by native First Nations residents, that park roads were once paved with them.

Vancouverites received a reminder that the earth is alive in 1980, when Mount St Helens in southern Washington erupted and spewed a film of fine ash over the city. One of Vancouver's most famous landmarks, Siwash Rock in Stanley Park, is the uneroded remnant of a small volcano within the city limits, and black volcanic rock underpins nearby Prospect Point. Volcanic rock was quarried for road material out of the city highpoint that today is Queen Elizabeth Park. Mount Garibaldi, a short drive east, was an active volcano 1,000 years ago. Constant landslides onto mountain roads are a regular reminder that geological processes work without pause.

Vancouver has even had several earthquakes. One in 1946 registered 7.3 on the Richter scale at the epicentre, which was fortunately some distance north. But buildings rocked, and the big clock on the Vancouver Block stopped. Minor earthquakes may cause some shaking. Seismologists say Vancouver and its environs are very likely to feel the impact of 'The Big One', if and when it comes.

Natural features

Each day, the sun sets over 6,500 islands, offshore from a rugged 27,000km (16,780-mile) coastline

BC – the ultimate temperate rainforest

indented by deep inlets. The magnificent Coast Mountains tower rank after rank in a northwest to southeast alignment. Eastwards, a broad plateau of rolling rangeland, mantled with moraines and other glacial deposits, stretches towards the thrusting snowy peaks of the Rocky Mountains. These form a natural barrier between BC and the rest of Canada, which is accessible by land via mountain passes at Crowsnest, Kicking Horse and Yellowhead. Kimberley, located at an altitude of 1,117m (3,665ft), is the highest city in Canada. North of the Rockies stretch the extensive fertile farmlands of the Peace River, a geographical continuation of the prairies.

The Fraser, Skeena, Nass, Stikine, Peace and Columbia Rivers weave a web of routes and barriers throughout the province. The earth varies from the silty soil of the Fraser delta and the Okanagan Valley to the barren, lichen-covered lava fields of Terrace. Subterranean volcanic activity produces thermal springs at Harrison, Halcyon, Radium and Fairmont, which are open to the public for warm mineral baths.

Precipitation varies with topography, from the permanently damp rainforests of Haida Gwaii (Queen Charlotte Islands) and frequent snowfalls of Mount Robson, the highest peak in the Canadian Rockies, to the sunny, arid Osoyoos desert with its cactuses, tumbleweed, sagebrush, lizards and rattlesnakes.

Taming the wilderness

Despite BC's vast and varied geography, man has made most areas accessible. A network of paved highways and railway tracks covers the countryside. The BC ferry fleet, one of the largest in the world, serves the islands and coastal towns, while in summer, luxury liners cruise to and from Alaska along the Inside Passage. International airports at Vancouver and Victoria, 350 other airfields and landing strips, and 100 seaplane bases permit access to remote regions. Forestry and allied industries, which employ 80,000 British Columbians, face stiff pressure from increasing world competition, which is eroding their traditional markets. Environmentalists, concerned over the future of the forests, have protested about how the forests are being managed.

Although timber, mining, agriculture and fishing all contribute to provincial coffers, tourism brings in substantial revenue. Visitors, who are mostly other Canadians, Americans, Britons, Japanese and Australians, often stay longer in BC than elsewhere in the country.

What nature has created, mankind has complemented with almost every conceivable recreational facility, resulting in a remarkable playground, especially in summer. More than 900 provincial parks, marine parks, and conservancies offer wilderness from thirty alpine lakes and five glaciers of Kokanee Glacier Provincial Park to the colourful underwater world of anemones, abalone and other aquatic creatures sought out by scuba divers along the coast.

Weather

If grey skies and wet weather are not for you, it is better to gamble on the drier and sunnier summer. From November to March, it is often dark and rainy. Some 178mm (7in) of rain drenches Vancouver in December,

Vancouver hosts a range of cultures

compared with 36mm (1½in) in July. The thermometer hovers around 22°C (72°F) in July and around 6°C (43°F) in December. Vancouver snows tend to be light and melt quickly. Winter rain downtown often means snow on the nearby mountains, so skiers can ski all day and evening and still get back downtown for a nightcap. Cool Pacific breezes make seashore strolls pleasant in summer. Now that wood and coal no longer heat homes, there is less smog, but an occasional patch of fog can slow drivers down in autumn. Although a haze may lay a thin grey or beige blanket over the city, most visitors find the air refreshing.

The climate is kind in Victoria and Vancouver. Resources are abundant. Yet most of the wilderness remains wilderness.

The people

BC is culturally complex. An increasing variety of people have come to live in Vancouver during the past few decades with the result an exhilarating mixture. Immigrants from Hong Kong, Taiwan, Japan, Vietnam and the Philippines in Asia, from Ethiopia, South Africa and Nigeria in Africa, from the USA, from many European countries and from Australasia have transformed the city. Everywhere, little neighbourhoods with a concentration of people from a single culture are popping up; most of the world is represented in the restaurants offering international cuisine, and in shops selling souvenirs and *objets d'art.*

Land and people

History

13 June 1792 Captain George Vancouver, exploring the Pacific Coast of North America, enters a body of water he names Burrard's Channel. Today, known as Burrard Inlet, it is the busy Vancouver Harbour.

2 July 1808 Simon Fraser, seeking fur-trading routes, arrives at Musqueam at the mouth of the Fraser River, where the native people chase him and his men back upstream.

1846 After a long territorial dispute, the Oregon Treaty is signed by Britain and the USA, placing BC in Canada.

2 August 1858 Following the discovery of gold on the Fraser River, American miners begin to pour in. The British Parliament passes an act establishing the mainland colony of BC. The colony of Vancouver Island already exists.

25 November 1858 Colonel Richard Moody arrives with a company of 'sappers' (soldier engineers) and begins building roads. The first road built still exists, as North Road, now the boundary between the Vancouver suburbs of Burnaby and Coquitlam.

26 September 1862 The McCleery family become the first settlers in Vancouver when they occupy land on the north bank of the Fraser River on what is now McCleery Golf Course.

October 1862 Three new arrivals from England, John Morton, Samuel Brighouse and William Hailstone, file a claim on 202 hectares (500 acres) on Burrard Inlet. The land is empty, swampy forest, so other colonists laughingly call them 'The Three Greenhorns'. Today, that land, the city's apartment-crammed West End, is worth billions.

June 1863 A sawmill, the first industry in the area, is established on the north shore of Burrard Inlet.

30 September 1867	'Gassy' Jack Deighton, so nicknamed because he talked incessantly, builds a saloon in 24 hours with the help of thirsty sawmill workers. The area around his saloon becomes known as Gastown.
1869–70	Gastown gets a jail … and the name Granville.
20 July 1871	BC joins the Confederation of Canada, formed in 1867.
6 April 1886	The City of Vancouver, renamed from Granville, is incorporated.
13 June 1886	The Great Fire destroys most buildings in the new little city, and 20 people die. Rebuilding begins at once.
23 May 1887	The first Canadian Pacific Railway (CPR) passenger train arrives in Vancouver; Vancouver's growth begins to accelerate.
1902	Vancouver's population reaches 30,000. Charles Woodward opens Vancouver's first department store.
1904	The Great Northern Railway reaches Vancouver.
1908	The University of BC is founded, which today has 50,000 students.
1913	The World Building is completed, the tallest in the British Empire at the time. Today, known as the Old Sun Tower, it looks rather modest.
28 August 1915	The first Canadian Northern Pacific Railway train arrives in Vancouver. Later, the line becomes known as the Canadian National Railway (CNR).
1 November 1919	The CNR Station opens. Today, it is the terminal for VIA Rail.
1 January 1929	On amalgamation with two adjacent municipalities, Vancouver becomes Canada's third-largest city, with nearly one-quarter of a million people.
22 July 1931	Vancouver Airport and Seaplane Harbour officially open.
4 December 1936	Vancouver's City Hall opens.
25 May 1939	The third, and present, Hotel Vancouver opens on

its present site, just a few days before King George VI and Queen Elizabeth stay there. The city names its newest park Queen Elizabeth Park.

6 August 1940	Theatre Under The Stars begins in Stanley Park, a much-loved tradition.
9 October 1944	The *St Roch*, a vessel operated by the Royal Canadian Mounted Police, arrives back in Vancouver from Halifax, having gone through the Northwest Passage in both directions. Shortly afterwards, the *St Roch* sails through the Panama Canal, becoming the first ship to circumnavigate North America.
15 July 1959	Queen Elizabeth and Prince Philip officiate at the opening of the Deas Island Tunnel, now called the Massey Tunnel.
9 September 1965	Simon Fraser University opens.
27 October 1984	The last sail is affixed on the development at Canada Place; the building,

designed by architect Eberhard Zeidler, is used for Expo '86 Canada Pavilion and later as one of Vancouver's two ship terminals, with another ship berth added in 2001.

1986	Expo '86, marking Vancouver's centennial, attracts 21 million visitors in six months and puts Vancouver in the world spotlight.
21 April 2001	Female orca Bjossa, the last live killer whale at the Vancouver Aquarium, moves to SeaWorld in San Diego, California.
23 January 2006	The Conservative Party wins the general election.
24 January 2009	The 62-storey Shangri-La, with a hotel and condos, opens and dominates Vancouver's skyline.
February & March 2010	Vancouver and Whistler host the 2010 Winter Olympic and Paralympic Games.
2017	Canada celebrates the 150th anniversary of confederation.

Politics

Canada is a confederation with a parliamentary democracy. In the federal general election of January 2006, the Conservatives led by Stephen Harper gained enough votes to form a minority government, ending eight years of rule by the middle-of-the-road Liberal Party, headed by Jean Chrétien.

BC's turbulent politics are a source of constant astonishment and amusement to the rest of the country (there are ten provinces in Canada, of which BC is one, and three territories, one of which, Nunavut, is administered by Inuit people).

From 1991 to 2001, the New Democrats held power. In 2000, Ujjal Dosanjh, an Indo-Canadian, replaced Glen Clark as the leader of the NDP and became Premier of BC. In May 2001, the Liberal Party won the provincial election and its leader, Gordon Campbell, a former Vancouver mayor, became Premier of the province – he was also re-elected in 2005 and 2009. The ratio of women and university graduates in local politics is now the highest in BC's history.

The province's lively political scene is reflected in microcosm in Vancouver, its largest city. For years, left-leaning members of the city council have been engaged in an ideological battle with the right. In the 2005 city elections, Sam Sullivan, a quadriplegic and active city councillor for years, became mayor, followed by Gregor Robertson in 2008, an organic juice company owner elected on a promise to 'green' Vancouver.

BC's 19th-century Parliament Buildings

Culture and events

Vancouver plays host to a full programme of festivals, exhibitions, sporting events and other special celebrations. Most of them are concentrated in the summer, but there is hardly a month of the year when there isn't something special going on. For more information, contact Tourism Vancouver (tel: (604) 683 2000; www.tourismvancouver.com).

In a vibrant city like Vancouver, there's an opportunity to enjoy a range of cultural events and celebrations.

FESTIVALS AND SPECIAL EVENTS
January
Polar Bear Swim
Every New Year's Day Vancouverites and visitors plunge into the chilly winter waters of English Bay.

Chinese New Year
A colourful celebration of old and modern traditions by Vancouver's Asian community, highlighted by the Dragon Parade in Chinatown (end January–beginning February).

March
Vancouver Playhouse International Wine Festival (Vancouver Convention Centre)
Features international wines for tastings, seminars and gala events (late March–early April).

May
The Cloverdale Rodeo
One of the largest rodeos on the continent, held at the fairgrounds over Victoria Day (24 May or preceding weekend).

Vancouver International Children's Festival (Vanier Park)
A sea of candy-striped tents transforms the park into a wonderland of theatre, music, puppetry and acrobatics.

Vancouver International Marathon
Runners from all over the world compete.

June
Rio Tinto Alcan Dragon Boat Festival
A weekend of racing, food and entertainment.

Vancouver International Jazz Festival
Big names in jazz perform at venues in and around the city. Gastown has a

two-day New Orleans-style street festival, one of the more popular events (late June–early July).

Bard on the Beach Shakespeare Festival
Different beach venues (June–September).

July
Canada Day
Entertainment and a spectacular fireworks show centred in Canada Place (1 July).

Dancing on the Edge Festival
A ten-day dance festival, with multiple venues.

HSBC Celebration of Light
A spectacular international fireworks competition over English Bay.

Vancouver Folk Music Festival
Three days of performances by local and international singers, musicians and storytellers at Jericho Beach Park.

August
Abbotsford Air Show (Abbotsford Airport)
Aerial acrobatics, skydiving and wing-walkers fill the skies.

September
Mid-Autumn Moon Festival
A Chinese cultural celebration at Dr Sun Yat-Sen Chinese Garden.

Vancouver International Comedy Festival
Comic performers from around the world at Granville Island.

Vancouver International Film Festival
One of the country's best (late September–mid-October).

Vancouver International Fringe Festival
Vancouver's theatre festival features 80 groups from around the world.

Victoria Classic Boat Festival
Admire wooden boats competing for recognition and watch a classic rowing regatta.

November
Heritage Christmas
Seasonal decorations and crafts at the Burnaby Village Museum (late November–early January).

December
Carol Ships Parade of Lights
Greater Vancouver boat-owners sail in the harbour in decorated craft.

Christmas at Canada Place
Santa and a light show on the pier's landmark sails, in support of local children's charities.

Festival of Lights
The central areas of VanDusen Garden are ablaze with lights.

Impressions

'You think BC means Before Christ. But it doesn't. I'm sitting, wildly surmising, on the edge of the Pacific, gazing at mountains which are changing colour every two minutes in the most surprising way. Nature here is half-Japanese.'

RUPERT BROOKE

English poet, 1913

What to bring

Vancouver is such a meeting ground of East and West and of business and sports, that almost any wardrobe is acceptable on any occasion, but check first if dining at a fine restaurant. Some women wear fox fur jackets and sandals to the office, while others wear parkas and running shoes. Shorts for both sexes are fine as leisurewear in summer, but a sweater is often welcome after the sun sets over the Pacific. An umbrella, raincoat and water-resistant footwear can be useful any time of the year, but more so in winter. Layered clothes are practical for trekking up the North Shore Mountains or for boating. Don't worry if you haven't brought what you need, for practically everything is sold here, and Canadian outdoor clothing and equipment are of excellent quality. Clothes are generally more expensive than in the USA, but cheaper than in Europe.

Driving and parking

More than 80 per cent of the travellers in BC are motorists. Driving is on the right, with passing on the left. Right turns are permitted on red lights, after the vehicle has come to a full stop. Pedestrians have the right of way on zebra crossings. City streets, freeways and country roads are well maintained.

Vancouver is becoming more crowded. Rush hour seems longer and parking downtown is challenging. Many parking meters are restricted during rush hours. There are plenty of big car parks (parkades) indoors and out, but on busy

Coal Harbour

The traditional Vancouver cab

days it may take a while to find a space. To Europeans, Vancouver drivers may seem almost archaically sedate, Victorians even more so, although driving manners are becoming less cautious. The use of seat belts is mandatory and, for motorcyclists and bike riders, helmets are life-saving and legally required.

Local customs

Some of the dour Scots who once settled this area had a reputed legacy of appearing unapproachable. Perhaps there is a remnant of the Wild West, where any stranger was subject to suspicion. An influx of residents from all over the world and athletes and visitors for the 2010 Winter Olympics has meant contact with unfamiliar traditions and exposure to new ideas. Vancouverites at first encounter may seem reluctant to be the first to say hello. A smile from friendly people goes a long way; so does 'I'm sorry' as a way of covering awkwardness when what's expected is not clear. Yet, the doorman at almost every downtown hotel will

accept a $5 tip and ease your way by keeping your car nearby for you at no additional charge.

Vancouver is an orderly city. People usually queue patiently at bus stops and taxi stands. Pedestrians use zebra crossings, as they have the right of way at intersections. Drivers rarely honk their horns, a ticketable offence, even when the traffic is almost reminiscent of downtown Bangkok at rush hour. If you ask for directions, remember that streets are usually referred to by just the main part of the name – 'Seymour Street' will therefore be known as 'Seymour'; similarly, North Vancouver is 'North Van'.

Smoking on the street, once considered bad form, is now more common. Smoking is not allowed in any fully or substantially enclosed public spaces, including workplaces, or within 3m (3¼yd) of their doorways or windows – that includes restaurants and drinking establishments. If in doubt, ask if and where smoking is permitted.

Totem poles in Stanley Park

distinguish the locals: they're often the pedestrians without umbrellas.

Many visitors find green zones like Stanley Park and the great patches of wilderness in Greater Vancouver, particularly on the North Shore, more than adequate for a short visit. But travellers seeking solitude may want to head into the hinterland where nature's creations are unspoilt.

Areas of BC
Cariboo Chilcotin Coast
This region stretches from the fjords of the Pacific and many offshore islands to the forested foothills of the Cariboo Mountains, with Gold Rush Trail history, volcanic landscapes, sand dunes, Fraser River white water and alpine vistas.

Kootenay Rockies
Four Canadian Rockies national parks – Glacier, Kootenay, Mount Revelstoke and Yoho – along with Kokanee Glacier Provincial Park, ring this region's northeast side. Stretching northwest from the 49th parallel near the Alberta border, the highway follows the Columbia River through the broad valley of the Rocky Mountain Trench, then joins TransCanada Highway 1 to continue west. Winter sports resorts spread along the east–west Crowsnest Highway (3).

Northern British Columbia
This vast area encompasses one-half of BC's land mass and stretches across the

Canadian couples are used to sleeping in double beds, but many rooms have two beds for the asking. Vancouverites usually eat salads before the main course, and green, Caesar and Greek salads are very popular. BC produces some excellent wines, so Vancouverites may favour BC labels over imported wines. Beer is a popular choice – look for a brewery on the premises. When the sun is out, outside patio dining and picnics are close by.

Few Vancouver residents venture into the great outdoors during the darker, rainy days of winter, though some jog compulsively right through thunderstorms without losing pace. In the rain, it is a little easier to

province from the Rockies to Haida Gwaii (Queen Charlotte Islands) First Nations culture and rainforest. In the northeast, from the Peace River Valley to the Rockies, the Alaska Highway runs from Dawson Creek (Mile Zero) northwest through Fort Nelson and Liard Valley to Alaska. In the northwest, the Stewart-Cassiar Highway (37) goes north to the Yukon and Alaska; grizzly bears have their own sanctuary in the Khutzeymateen Valley.

Thompson Okanagan

The Okanagan Valley, situated north of the American border midway between the Rockies and the Pacific, produces much of BC's wines and fruit. Between the Cascade and Monashee Mountain Ranges, the region includes Shuswap and Nicola Lakes and the Canadian Rockies' highest peak, Mount Robson.

Vancouver, coast and mountains

Vancouver, its suburbs to the US border, the Sunshine Coast, Hell's Gate and the Fraser River, and Whistler's craggy mountain peaks lure visitors to this accessible and populated region.

Vancouver Island

The long western island off the BC mainland includes the provincial capital, Victoria, wild western shoreline, whale-watching, First Nations' heritage, luxury resorts, farms, murals, artisan food producers and artists. The region includes a small mainland section and the ferry-ride-close Gulf Islands, a getaway for urbanites, especially in summer.

Coastline along the Wild Pacific Trail

Areas of Vancouver

Greater Vancouver is bounded by the North Shore Mountains, the Strait of Georgia to the west and the American border to the south. As more people move to the city, the fertile farmlands of the Fraser Valley to the east are fast being replaced by suburban development.

Downtown Vancouver

In addition to the main business and shopping area, the city centre has several different sections. **Gastown**, the renovated original part of the city, contains souvenir shops, restaurants and art galleries. **Robson Street** has several blocks of upmarket shops and restaurants; there are high-end art galleries along South Granville Street. **Chinatown** has a colourful collection of shops and restaurants especially lively at weekends. **Yaletown** is an area of old warehouses, renovated to house restaurants, galleries and studios of artists, architects and designers. **Granville Island**, reached by water taxi, has the Public Market, Maritime Market, art galleries and artists.

With large-scale immigration, ethnic enclaves have developed in Vancouver, and shops and restaurants cater to their tastes. There are east Indians along the southern end of Main Street, Greeks along West Broadway, Germans on Fraser Street and Italians on Commercial Drive, and around Hastings and Nanaimo Streets. There is a tiny Japantown on Powell Street and an equally small French-language pocket on West 16th Avenue.

Kerrisdale

Gentrification in recent years has polished the image of this neighbourhood south of Kitsilano.

Kitsilano

Kitsilano, especially along West Fourth Avenue, was once a hotbed of the hippy era, with its pot-smokers, tie-dyers, vegetarians, protesters and peaceniks. It still remains the most laid-back neighbourhood in town.

Shaughnessy

In this wealthy neighbourhood, streets lined with towering trees curve around imposing mansions. Shaughnessy was established by the Canadian Pacific Railway a century ago as a residential enclave for executives.

Suburbia

Nearly two dozen suburbs surround Vancouver. **Richmond**, the site of Vancouver International Airport, is a thriving city to the south with a large Asian-heritage population. **Surrey**, a huge municipality on the south side of the Fraser River, is also expanding fast. The southern part of Surrey is very attractive, with dairy farms dotted around the green, rolling hills. Posh **West Vancouver**, a quiet, high-income residential area, has some of the most agreeable suburbs.

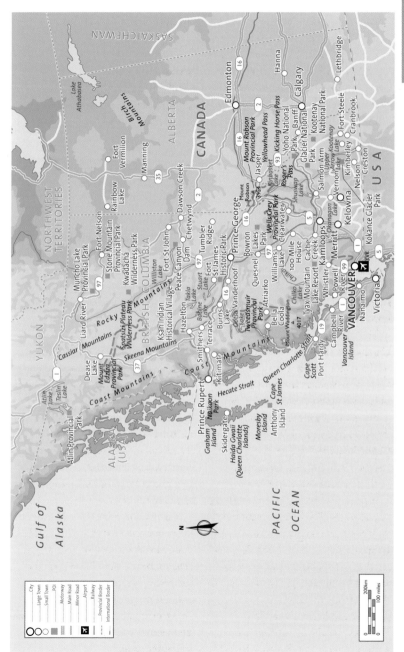

Vancouver

Vancouver, commonly called the Gateway to the Pacific, is almost entirely surrounded by water. To the north is Burrard Inlet, an ice-free harbour where freighters fly the flags of many nations. To the south, the Fraser River flows west into the Strait of Georgia, which separates the mainland from Vancouver Island. The sheltering ranges attract grey clouds that shower the city with 140cm (55in) of rain a year, resulting in lush green landscapes. The clouds frost the peaks with snow for skiing five months a year.

Metropolitan Vancouver covers 2,878sq km (1,111sq miles), including the suburbs of North Vancouver, West Vancouver, Burnaby, Coquitlam, Port Coquitlam, Port Moody, Pitt Meadows, Richmond, White Rock, Delta, New Westminster, Surrey and Langley.

Although Vancouver is Canada's third-largest city (after Toronto and Montreal), its many waterways, mountains and parks lend the city an illusion of space.

Mounties are everywhere!

While the past has largely been a story of seeking and selling natural resources, new industries are emerging. Local skills now produce sightseeing submarines, satellite-sensing equipment, computer software and data terminal designs.

A growing tourism industry draws some visitors back as residents. Hotels continue to spring up in a city centre of skyscrapers. Well-developed facilities and roadways allow visitors and residents to ski in the morning, sail in the afternoon and enjoy opera in the evening. Even business seems a sport in this city, which has one of the most speculative stock markets in the world.

Most people come to Vancouver for the scenery, so first select one of its many vantage points for an overview of the city. People who like to keep their feet firmly planted on the ground may prefer to stroll along the promenade walkway at **Canada Place Pier**, a good orientation spot. With its five white sails jutting out into the harbour, this

Downtown Vancouver

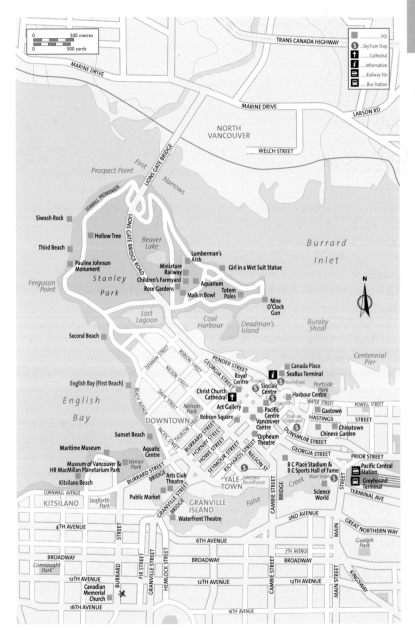

city landmark features a dozen markers indicating sites of interest around the city. You can also enjoy spectacular views from some downtown city buildings, or take an aerial tour and get a real bird's-eye view.

THE CITY FROM ABOVE
Aerial sightseeing
Harbour Air
BC's largest seaplane company packages eight tours, varying from a half-hour flight over the city centre to a six-hour round trip to Vancouver Island.
Tel: (604) 274 1277, freephone (800) 665 0212; www.harbour-air.com

Helijet
Scenic city and wilderness tours, departing from downtown and Grouse Mountain. Options range from the 20-minute West Coast Spectacular to a Coastal Scenic or Greater Vancouver Tour. Some tours are seasonal, May to September, and weather dependent.
Tel: (604) 270 1484,

freephone (800) 665 4354; www.helijet.com

Sea to Sky Air
The company operates spectacular air tours over Vancouver. Other plane and helicopter tours explore Whistler and Squamish.
Tel: (604) 898 1975; www.seatoskyair.ca

Sundance Balloons
Early morning and sunset flights over BC landscapes with champagne. Flights run from May to October (as weather permits).
Tel: (604) 533 7552; www.sundanceballoons.com

Bird's-eye viewpoints
Cloud Nine
The price of a meal or a drink at the revolving Cloud 9 restaurant, atop the 42-storey Empire Landmark Hotel, includes a 360-degree view of Vancouver.
1400 Robson St. Tel: (604) 687 0511; www.cloud9restaurant.ca

The view across False Creek

Harbour Centre

Get your bearings from above at Vancouver Lookout, a revolving viewing deck at the top of the Harbour Centre.

555 West Hastings St. Tel: (604) 689 0421; www.vancouverlookout.com. Open: daily summer 8.30am–10.30pm; winter 9am–9pm. Admission charge.

BEACHES

Although beachcombing is a pleasant pastime come rain or shine in winter, Vancouver beaches are at their best in summer. From Victoria Day to Labour Day, lifeguards supervise the city's ten swimming beaches from 11.30am to 8.30pm and to 9pm mid-June to mid-August. There is no admission charge to the beaches, and changing rooms, toilets and refreshment stands are found in many convenient locations.

English Bay (First Beach)

Fifteen minutes from downtown, English Bay sports some fine beaches.
Beach Ave between Gilford and Bidwell Sts.

Kitsilano Beach

Kitsilano Beach has a heated outdoor salt-water pool overlooking English Bay. Nearby Jericho Beach, Locarno Beach and Spanish Banks are favourites with windsurfers. There is adequate parking, and picnic tables are dotted along the beach.
North end of Yew St, west of the Burrard St Bridge.

Second Beach

This beach features a pool that protects children from the currents. There are areas for barbecues and for playing soccer, football, volleyball and baseball.
North Lagoon Dr, in Stanley Park, north of Sunset Beach.

Sunset Beach

At this beach, the closest to downtown, summer sunsets are glorious. Residents and visitors congregate on giant logs on the beach or sip sundowners at the front tables in the nearby Boathouse Restaurant and the Sylvia Hotel.
Beach Ave between Thurlow and Bute Sts.

Third Beach

This isolated beach is relatively quiet, a haven for those looking to get away.
On the west side of Stanley Park, north of Second Beach and Ferguson Point.

Wreck Beach

This beach has unrivalled natural beauty. A steep trail (not easy to find; ask for directions) winds down to the water from North West Marine Drive to this unspoilt wild strand, the only nudist beach in the Lower Mainland.
On the tip of the Point Grey Peninsula near the University of British Columbia.

For information, contact in season tel: (604) 738 8535, and off season tel: (604) 665 3424); http://vancouver.ca

The charm of Vancouver beaches

Vancouver's 18km (11 miles) of beaches are an essential part of the city's outdoor culture. They provide the perfect venue for cycling, rollerblading, beach volleyball, watching windsurfers and kayakers or, on a more relaxing note, a romantic stroll, and, of course, sunbathing.

On New Year's Day in Vancouver, around 2,000 locals dash into English Bay for the Polar Bear Swim. No one lingers long; they dress quickly and head indoors to recuperate from the chilling waters.

But summer is another story. The city's ten beaches become crowded with swimmers, sandcastle-builders, frisbee-players, kite-flyers and sun-seekers who want to have fun. An occasional canine slips in without

The beaches around the city provide idyllic recreational spaces for urbanites

Kitsilano Beach

permission, and squirrels sometimes appear hoping for handouts. There are three 'quiet' beaches: Locarno, Spanish Bank West, and Sunset, where amplified music is not allowed. Freshwater Trout Lake is also ringed by beach.

Although many people bring picnics, alcohol is not allowed. There are sandy, gravel and pebble shores. English Bay's Sunset Beach is ribboned with gigantic trunks from rainforest trees that escaped log booms, a reminder that timber was a key industry here. The logs are great for leaning on, and they provide some privacy. Some are big enough for a single sunbather to stretch right out on top.

Although the heat of the sun is tempered by refreshing offshore breezes, it is wise to wear a strong sunscreen for protection against the direct rays and those reflected off the sea and sand, and bring something to cover yourself up. West Vancouver's Ambleside Beach is one of the city beaches that permits barbecues. It is wonderful to roast hot dogs and marshmallows around a flickering fire as the Lions Gate Bridge lights up and the sunset fades into the darkening evening sky over English Bay.

CHINATOWN

Vancouver's thriving Chinatown, a ten-minute walk from the city centre, stretches over six blocks, north to south down Main Street to the Georgia Street viaduct, and east to west from Gore Street to Carrall and Taylor Streets. Millions of dollars change hands here, in hundreds of businesses ranging from banks to food to electronics. Another burgeoning community with Chinese heritage is in Vancouver's suburb Richmond.

Chinatown is home to a few thousand permanent residents. Most Chinese Canadians live elsewhere, but often come to Chinatown to bank, shop and eat. The streets bustle with activity. Shops overflowing with rosewood furniture, bamboo and wickerware, jade jewellery and porcelain stand cheek-by-jowl with herbal pharmacies and authentic Chinese restaurants, most of which serve excellent food at reasonable prices.

For more information:
www.vancouver-chinatown.com,
http://vcbia.brinkster.net,
http://vancouver.ca/commsvcs/planning/
heritage/walks/w_ch_map.htm

Chinese Cultural Centre

Situated between Carrall and Columbia Streets (*see p30*), the Chinese Cultural Centre houses changing exhibitions of traditional culture and local history and sponsors the annual Chinese New Year Parade.

50 East Pender St. Tel: (604) 658 8850;
www.cccvan.com. Open: Tue–Sun 9am–
5.30pm. Free admission.

Dr Sun Yat-Sen Chinese Garden

This garden (*see pp30–31*), opened for Expo '86, was created in classical Chinese style and is a harmonious blend of plants and space, with numerous terraces, pavilions and walkways.

578 Carrall St. Tel: (604) 662 3207;
www.vancouverchinesegarden.com.
Hours vary according to season; call for
open dates and times. Admission charge.

Sam Kee Building

See p30.
At the southwest corner of Pender and
Carrall Sts. Not open to the public, but
can be viewed from outside.

Gateway to Chinatown

GALLERIES

Vancouver is a young city, and youthful energy and enthusiasm are reflected in the freshness of its art scene, both in traditional West Coast art and in more avant-garde work. Since galleries often close to mount new shows and because some are staffed by volunteers, phone ahead to check opening times.

Downtown

Buschlen Mowatt Galleries

Dedicated to showcasing museum-quality contemporary artists of regional, national and international significance, with a focus on sculpture.
1445 West Georgia St.
Tel: (604) 682 1234;
www.buschlenmowatt.com

Dorian Rae Collection

Southeast Asian, West African and American Southwest art and artefacts.
410 Howe St. Tel: (604) 874 6100;
www.dorianraecollection.com

Rendezvous Art Gallery

Paintings and sculptures by emerging and established Canadian artists.
323 Howe St. Tel: (604) 687 7466;
www.rendezvousartgallery.com

Teck Gallery

Features changing exhibitions.
Simon Fraser University, Harbour Centre, 515 West Hastings St.
Tel: (778) 782 4266;
www.sfu.ca/artgallery

Vancouver Art Gallery

A neoclassical heritage building and a work of art itself, it houses paintings by the early 20th-century Canadian artists known as the Group of Seven; evocative rainforest works by Emily Carr (1871–1945); works by Dutch, Italian, French, German and English masters; and photography, sculpture, graphics and video works. You can wander around on your own or join a free tour on certain days. The reference-only library, gift shop and restaurant make the Vancouver Art Gallery a rainy-day special.
750 Hornby St.
Tel: (604) 662 4719
for 24-hour information;
www.vanartgallery.bc.ca

Gastown

Hill's Native Art

Art from Canada's First Nations artists in a variety of media – prints, carvings, totems, beadwork and more. Hill's will ship your purchases.
165 Water St. Tel: (866) 685 5422;
www.hillsnativeart.com

Inuit Gallery

Exhibits and sells excellent traditional Inuit masterworks, Cape Dorset Inuit sculpture and West Coast native Indian works.
206 Cambie St. Tel: (604) 688 7323;
www.inuit.com

Marion Scott Gallery

Features Inuit sculptures, prints, drawings and wall hangings.
308 Water St.
Tel: (604) 685 1934;
www.marionscottgallery.com

Walk: Chinatown

Vancouver's Chinatown (see also p28), the second largest in area in North America after San Francisco's, crams a lot of life into six city blocks, a ten-minute walk from the city centre.

Allow 2 hours for walking and another hour for dim sum (small bites of prepared food, served and paid for by the plate).

Begin this tour at the corner of Taylor and West Pender Sts.

1 Vancouver Chinatown Millennium Gate
Look for the triple pagoda-style gold tile roof atop this formal entrance at Taylor and West Pender Streets.

2 Sam Kee Building
Built in 1913 at 8 West Pender Street, the Sam Kee Building may be the

The Dr Sun Yat-Sen Chinese Garden, a taste of the Orient in Vancouver's Chinatown

narrowest building in the world (1.8m by 30m/6ft by 98ft), and is listed in *Guinness World Records*. The two-storey house is now private offices.

3 *Century's Winds of Change* Mural
On the side of a building at 11 West Pender Street is a mural depicting 100 years of Chinese presence in Canada.

4 Chinese Cultural Centre
In the next block at 50 East Pender Street, the Chinese Cultural Centre, marked by an enormous red gateway, houses a library and rooms for language lessons, t'ai chi, Chinese painting, lantern making and exhibits of oriental and Canadian art.

5 Dr Sun Yat-Sen Chinese Garden
High, whitewashed walls hide this pocket of peace at 578 Carrall Street near Keefer Street from the bustling city beyond. Modelled after the classic scholars' gardens of the Ming Dynasty

(1368–1644), the Taoist balance of yin and yang (light and shadow, smooth and rough, large and small) creates perfect harmony. This quiet, secluded sanctuary shelters vistas of pebbled patios, moon gates, lattice windows, see-through shrubbery, placid milky-jade pools and craggy grey limestone. *Return to East Pender St.*

6 Wing Sang Building

At 51–67 East Pender Street, the oldest standing structure in Chinatown dates from 1889.

7 Monument of Canadian Chinese

Cross East Pender and walk south on Columbia Street towards Keefer Street where bronze statues of a Chinese railway worker and Chinese Canadian World War II soldier flank a Chinese character for peace and harmony. *Retrace your steps to East Pender St.*

8 Pender Street

Both sides of Pender are lined with Mandarin, Cantonese and Szechuan restaurants, and shops selling such

NEARBY

Christ Church of China, Sun Tower

imported goods as wickerware, parasols, porcelain, bamboo birdcages, jade jewellery, attractive rosewood furniture, delicate porcelain, *cloisonné* and silk embroidery. Prices are reasonable, and browsers are welcome. Many stores will ship everything home for you. At the Chinese pharmacies, experts busily mix potions of herbs, cuttlefish, powdered antler velvet and other exotic ingredients to alleviate everything from influenza to impotence. *Cross Main St, still on Pender St, turn right on Gore Ave, walk a block to Keefer St and turn right again.*

9 Keefer Street

Here, the predominant aroma announces windows of Chinese pastries. Most pastry shops have a room at the back for a tasty cup of tea and a snack (be warned: the coffee is usually mediocre). *Follow Keefer St two blocks west back to the Dr Sun Yat-Sen Chinese Garden and the free Dr Sun Yat-Sen Park.*

Chinese Canadians

During the 5th century, several Chinese Buddhist priests visited a country they called Fu Sang, now believed to have been the West Coast of Canada. But the first real wave of Chinese immigrants did not arrive until the 1858 gold rush. Some stayed and started farms and laundries, or worked in the salmon canneries, sawmills and coal mines. Some 25 years later, 10,000 Chinese workers were imported to lay tracks for Canada's transcontinental railway. Continuing racism forced Chinese male workers and a few families to live crowded together in a small area centred on what was later named Pender Street, the beginning of today's Chinatown in Vancouver.

Without the right to vote and with frequent overt discrimination, Chinatown's population diminished. Canada's Exclusion Act barred new Chinese immigration in 1923–47. After World War II, when China had been Canada's ally, tension lessened and Chinatown became a favoured destination for Vancouverites. Chinese

Tranquillity in the middle of Vancouver's thriving Chinatown

Exotic ingredients await you in Chinatown

Canadians fought against a freeway through Chinatown in 1968, and in 1971, Vancouver designated Chinatown a historic district.

Some Hong Kong families, concerned about Hong Kong's return to China in 1997, sent their teenage offspring to study in Canadian schools and universities. Others invested in property, manufacturing, electronics and other ventures in preparation for future permanent residence in BC. The highest office in the province, that of Lieutenant-Governor, was held in 1988–95 by David Lam, a highly respected and admired Chinese immigrant.

Canada's latest Census (of 2006) showed that 402,000 of BC's 432,000 Chinese Canadians lived in Vancouver. Others have settled elsewhere in the province, particularly around Vancouver suburb Richmond's Golden Village, which may have overtaken Chinatown as North America's second largest after San Francisco's! Asian immigrants continue to arrive each year; more than 25 per cent of children entering school here speak Cantonese or Mandarin as their mother tongue, and Chinatown has its own graceful Monument of Canadian Chinese.

For more information contact the Chinese Cultural Centre Museum and Archives, *tel: (604) 658 8880; www.cccvan.com*

Walk: Gastown

Gastown, a five-minute hike from the city centre, is the oldest part of Vancouver. The area was designated a heritage site in 1971. Old gas-style lamps and young maple trees line cobblestoned Water St, whose three blocks constitute the heart of Gastown. For more information visit www.gastown.org

Allow at least 2 hours.

Begin this tour at the corner of Richards and Water Sts. Head east on the north side of Water St.

1 The Landing

The first stop, The Landing, is an award-winning heritage structure containing a dozen elegant shops clustered around a central lobby, whose arched floor-to-ceiling window frames the North Shore Mountains. A shiny escalator leads from one polished oak floor to the other. Head to the lower level, pick up a local newspaper or the *New York Times* at the Fleet Street newsstand, and savour a cappuccino and muffin, a good mélange of America and Europe, at the friendly café or a beer at the Steamworks, restaurant for the onsite Gastown Brewing Company. Landmark shops sell Scottish tartans, Belgian chocolates, Japanese lingerie, cut and potted flowers, Canadian winter clothes, gold jewellery handcrafted on-site, designer clothes, toys for children, embroidered Victoria cushions, maple-wood salad bowls and smoked salmon packed for shipping. *Continue along Water St.*

2 Inuit Gallery

Water Street is lined with dozens of shops selling everything from souvenir sweatshirts to Art Deco furniture. The most exciting stop is the Inuit Gallery, a few doors east of The Landing, which houses an impressive array of Inuit sculpture and Northwest Coast native art. So-called 'naive' art recalls the way Inuit families used to live in harmony with their harsh land, expressed in soapstone and whalebone sculptures. The shop also sells Northwest Native Canadian cedar carvings, buttoned blankets and ceremonial masks.
A little further along on the left is the Steam Clock.

3 Steam Clock

Dedicated to the citizens of Vancouver in 1977, the 2-ton Steam Clock was built by Gillett & Johnston of Croydon,

England. Their clock movement was based on an 1875 vintage design, and has a 19kg (42lb) gold-plated pendulum.

A machine in a nearby basement is triggered by clockwork every 15 minutes, and pins play a tune that electronically blows five steam whistles. A 24-carat gold-plated frame surrounds the dials, which glow at night.
Continue along Water St.

4 The Courtyard

In the next block meander through The Courtyard, where Vancouver architects, tour operators and lawyers work behind huge glass windows. The outdoor café and delicatessen up the stairs provides a pleasant pause with a view across the harbour.
At the end of Water St, turn right into Carrall St.

5 Maple Tree Square

In Maple Tree Square stands the statue of 'Gassy' Jack Deighton, a garrulous

Yorkshireman who built a saloon for lumber mill workers on the site of the Broghes building behind in 1867.

The building is made with bricks from China that were used as ballast on sailing ships calling for timber at the Hastings Mill. Deighton, who had arrived in Vancouver with his wife, six dollars, a few sticks of furniture and a yellow dog, was an overnight success. Because he was so talkative and optimistic about prospects for Burrard Inlet, locals called him 'Gassy Jack', and the ramshackle collection of huts and shops surrounding the saloon was dubbed Gastown. Jack's statue faces the old Europe Hotel, a good example of the renovated Victorian buildings in Gastown.
Turn west through the Gaoler's Mews.

6 Gaoler's Mews

This cobblestoned courtyard is where Vancouver's first gaol once stood. A little further along, Blood Alley marks the site of many dastardly deeds during the settlement of the Wild West.

The south side of Water Street is also lined with shops and restaurants. Water Street restaurants cover the cuisines of Italy, France, Ethiopia, India and America. Just off Water Street at 217 Carrall, you'll find The Irish Heather, a gastropub serving its version of Irish food.
Return along Water St to The Landing.

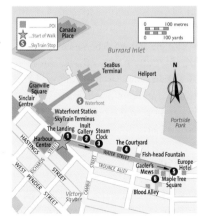

NEARBY

Portside Park, Harbour Centre

Tour: Vancouver Trolley

The Trolley Tour provides the best preview of Vancouver's varied attractions. The bright red-and-gold non-polluting gas-operated trolleys, decorated in oak and brass, are replicas of those used in the 1890s. There are two loops that make stops, many of them at major hotels. Both loops begin and end at Canada Place, but you can start your tour anywhere on the trolley line.

Allow about 2 hours for both loop tours if you don't take advantage of the stops.

1 Canada Place
Promenade beneath the sails at Canada Place Pier.

BLUE LOOP
2 Marriott Pinnacle/ Renaissance Hotel

3 Hyatt Regency/Melville Street
Two blocks from Robson Street's lively shopping district.

4 Vancouver Art Gallery (Howe), Pacific Centre
Among other works, the Vancouver Art Gallery houses a large collection of paintings by renowned local artist and author Emily Carr.

5 Holiday Inn (Helmcken)

6 Quality Inn (Drake)

7 Vanier Park
For the Museum of Vancouver, Vancouver Maritime Museum and H R MacMillan Space Centre.

8 Granville Island (entrance)
Walk to where arts, industry and dining are side by side in this colourful market district.
The trolley goes over the Burrard St Bridge back towards downtown.

9 Yaletown (Roundhouse)
Vancouver's trendy designer district. High-end shopping and dining.

10 Edgewater Casino

11 Library Square (Homer)
This distinctive complex houses government offices, the main library, shopping and cafés.

12 Dr Sun Yat-Sen Chinese Garden/Chinatown
Eat, shop and enjoy the classic Chinese

garden in Vancouver's compact Chinatown (*see pp30–31*).

13 Police Museum (E Cordova)

North of Chinatown in the historic Coroner's Court.

14 The Old Spaghetti Factory (Gastown)

15 Gastown/Steam Clock

The heart of old Vancouver and home to the Steam Clock (*see pp34–5*).

16 Waterfront Station/SeaBus Terminal/Vancouver Lookout

Hop on one of Vancouver's passenger ferries or head up to Vancouver Lookout to see the metropolis from above.

RED LOOP
2 Robson Street (Blue Horizon Hotel)

Tourists and locals alike promenade Robson to take advantage of the street's varied shopping.

3 Westin Bayshore Resort

After the Westin the trolley enters Stanley Park. The route goes around the outside of the park and stops at all the major attractions.

4 Stanley Park: Rose Gardens

The Rose Gardens are at their showiest between June and October and in late March and April.

5 Stanley Park: Aquarium

Visit the Vancouver Aquarium to see the beluga whales.

6 Stanley Park: Totem poles

A stunning introduction to the history and culture of British Columbia's First Nations people.

7 Stanley Park: Prospect Point

Admire the view from Prospect Point.

8 & 9 Stanley Park: Teahouse and Fish House Restaurants

Request a stop for a bite to eat at one of Stanley Park's fine restaurants. *The trolley leaves Stanley Park at English Bay.*

10 English Bay

Popular for sunbathing, beautiful sunset views, and dining.

11 False Creek Ferries

Go to Granville Island by water or up False Creek to the child-friendly Science Centre.

12 Cascadia Hotel

13 Sheraton Wall Centre Hotel

Tours run mid-April to late October. Call or check online for tour times and last stops at various locations. Vancouver Trolley offers other themed tours – contact it for tickets and information (tel: (604) 801 5515, freephone (888) 451 5581; www.vancouvertrolley.com).

Tour: Vancouver Trolley

Granville Island

Charles H Scott Gallery
Located in the Emily Carr University of Art + Design, the gallery mounts travelling shows. Walk through the school and look at students' work.
1399 Johnston St. Tel: (604) 844 3809;
http://chscott.ecuad.ca

Federation of Canadian Artists
Juried exhibits of original paintings by Canadian artists.
1241 Cartwright St. Tel: (604) 681 8534;
http://artists.ca

Lattimer Gallery
Sells many current works by First Nations artists.
1590 W 2nd Ave. Tel: (604) 732 4556;
www.lattimergallery.com

South Granville

Bau-Xi Gallery
Features Canadian contemporary art. Be sure to look upstairs.
3045 Granville St.
Tel: (604) 733 7011;
www.bau-xi.com

Diane Farris Gallery
Contemporary painting and sculpture from up-and-comers to established artists.
1590 W 7th Ave. Tel: (604) 737 2629;
www.dianefarrisgallery.com

Douglas Reynolds Gallery
Historical and contemporary First Nations masks, jewellery, prints and other fine arts.
2335 Granville St.
Tel: (604) 731 9292;
www.douglasreynoldsgallery.com

Equinox Gallery
Features international contemporary shows.
2321 Granville St.
Tel: (604) 736 2405;
www.equinoxgallery.com

Petley Jones Gallery
Features contemporary and older works in dealer's stock.
2235 Granville St.
Tel: (604) 732 5353;
www.petleyjones.com

Other galleries

Canoe Pass Gallery
Gifted Canadian native artists.
115–3866 Bayview St,
Steveston Village, Richmond.
Tel: (604) 272 0095;
www.canoepass.com

Catriona Jeffries
Exhibits and sells interesting contemporary local and imported art.
274 E 1st Ave.
Tel: (604) 736 1554;
www.catrionajeffries.com

Surrey Art Gallery
An eclectic programme of temporary exhibitions alongside its permanent collection.
13750 88th Ave, Surrey.
Tel: (604) 501 5566; www.surrey.ca

Western Front
The premier multi-discipline gallery in Canada, with artist-managed gallery space.
303 E 8th Ave.
Tel: (604) 878 7563;
www.front.bc.ca

GARDENS AND PARKS

Every February, when most of Canada is still covered in ice and snow, the first crocuses of spring poke their heads above ground to take a look at Vancouver and Victoria. The temperate coastal climate, ample sunshine and abundant rainfall encourage and ensure a great diversity of colourful flora. The greenery, which reigns supreme most of the year, is upstaged by riots of colourful blossom in spring and summer.

There are more than 150 gardens and parks in Vancouver, not counting the hundreds of thousands of private yards and gardens. Two of the prettiest public oases in the city differ greatly in character. Wild and rambling Stanley Park (*see pp63–4*) is Western, while the Dr Sun Yat-Sen Chinese Garden (*see pp30–31*) is typically Eastern.

Nitobe Memorial Garden

Reflecting the private retreats of Japan, gentle walkways meander through artistically pruned cherry, maple and pine trees, and layouts of sand and rock, to a tiny tea house. The cherry blossoms in April or May and the late June iris bloom are spectacular.
Across the street from the UBC Botanical Garden. Tel: (604) 822 4208; www.nitobe.org. Open: daily. Admission charge.

Park and Tilford Gardens

This privately owned eight-garden area offers a delightful variety of plantings and landscape themes, including a White Garden and an Oriental Garden.
333 Brooksbank Ave, North Vancouver. Tel: (604) 984 8200; www. parkandtilford.ca/pandtgardens.htm. Open: daily 9am–dusk. Free admission.

Queen Elizabeth Park

This 53-hectare (130-acre) former stone quarry, transformed into sunken gardens, is a favourite site for bridal couples and wedding photos amid lawns, trees, shrubs and flowers. At 153m (50ft), the park is the highest spot in the city, so views are spectacular. The blossoms are at their best in late May and June, when azaleas and rhododendrons create a brilliant kaleidoscope of colour. An arboretum on the east side showcases trees and shrubs indigenous to the BC coast.

There is also a rose garden, a pitch-and-putt golf course (*tel: (604) 874 8336*), 18 tennis courts, t'ai chi arbours, a dancing (water) fountain and Seasons in the Park restaurant looking out to the city. The Bloedel Floral Conservatory (*tel: (604) 257 8584*), a 20m (65ft) high triodetic dome, houses a tropical garden with more than 100 colourful birds flying free, and an arid area with cacti, and seasonal floral displays.
33rd Ave and Cambie St. Tel: (604) 257 8570; http://vancouver.ca/parks/parks/queenelizabeth. Open: mid-Apr–Sept daily 9am–8pm; Oct–mid-Apr
(Cont. on p44)

Walk: Art in public places

Vancouver's neighbourhoods are full of outdoor art and exceptional architecture. A walk along the waterfront at English Bay or the False Creek side of the city reveals diverse works – fountains, sculpture in a variety of media, architecture from Art Deco to postmodern … View Vancouver's public art collection with descriptions and photographs online: http://vancouver.ca. *The city has a detailed guide that takes sturdy walkers 13km (8 miles) around the perimeter of downtown.*

A plan of the entire walk, with a map, is available at http://vancouver.ca/commsvcs/oca/publicart/pdf/Shoreline Walk.PDF. Less ambitious art-lovers may want to focus only on a specific district.

The walk's first 12 stops are along the waterfront at Burrard Inlet. Start in Coal Harbour on the Canada Place Pier.

1 Canada Place

With its soaring, sail-like roof, this was the Expo '86 Canada Pavilion. Information panels retell the area's history – don't overlook the stunning views.

2 *Salute to the Lions of Vancouver*

On the west side of Canada Place are Gathie Falk's two leaping lions, which reflect the Lions Gate Bridge and the Lions Mountains, known to local First Nations as the Two Sisters.
Cross the street and walk up the pedestrian area to Hornby St.

3 *Working Landscape*

Three rotating platforms by Daniel Laskarin complete their full revolutions in one-hour, eight-hour and 40-hour increments.
Head down Hastings towards Burrard St.

4 Marine Building

The Marine Building at 355 Burrard Street is an Art Deco gem, built in 1930 with sea-life- or bird-inspired surface decorations in the entrance and elaborate lift doors.

5 *Public Service/Private Steps*

Alan Storey's *Public Service/Private Steps* is at 401 Burrard, just across Hastings from the Marine Building. The moving cubes mimic the activity of the people and the lifts inside the building.

6 Harbour Green Shoreline

Stroll down the waterfront and enjoy this sea wall park designed to be an expanding home for public art – look for Liz Magor's *Light Shed* and Dan Corson's *One in Light* – a fountain that reflects changing colours at night.

7 Weave

At the foot of Jervis Street towards the west end of the park, look down to find one component of *Weave* by Douglas Senft. The rings represent the staggering size of old-growth trees. *Weave* includes other references to British Columbia's natural history.

8 Make West

Along Coal Harbour Quay between Nicola Street and Cardero, Bill Pechet's *Make West* re-creates the history of Coal Harbour with a series of stones, plaques and bronze castings set in the walkway.

9 Bayshore Waterfront Walkway and Gardens

Just north of the Westin Bayshore Hotel, look for the steel and glass

shelters that reroute rainwater back to the inlet. Take a break on one of the benches in this plaza and enjoy the views and the gardens.

10 Leaf Stream

A few steps further down the walkway is *Leaf Stream*, Douglas Senft's cascading fountain at the foot of Georgia Street. The water flows over recognisable Canada icons – bronze maple leaves.

11 Search

Enter Devonian Park at the foot of Denman Street and have a seat next to the subject of S Seward Johnson Jr's *Search*.

12 Solo

End this portion of the walk at *Solo*, also in Devonian Park. This abstract piece by Natalie McHaffie expresses motion in shiny stainless steel.

Walk: Art in public places

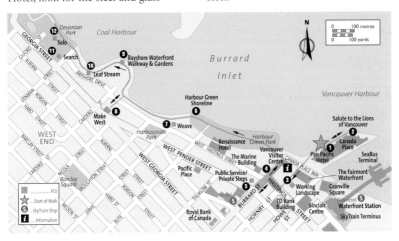

The BC art scene

Nature has been and continues to be the dominating influence motivating local artists. It is clearly evident in their work, from the powerful and mysterious moods of old-growth rainforests and totem poles painted by Emily Carr to the subtle watercolour seascapes of Toni Onley.

Emily Carr, born in Victoria in 1871, is acknowledged as the grand matriarch of BC art. Her inspiration came from both the natural surroundings and the original inhabitants, as she travelled the BC coast collecting and portraying a wealth of impressions from

The Raven and the First Men by Bill Reid

Visit Vancouver Art Gallery on Robson Square

First Nations peoples, their arts and their legends.

Other BC greats include Bill Reid, Reg Davidson and Roy Vickers, who all have a native heritage; European immigrants John Coerner from the former Czechoslovakia, and Bratsa Bonisacho from the former Yugoslavia; Attila Rick Lukacs, originally from Alberta; as well as other talents such as Ross Penhall and Lorraine Yabuki.

Since the 1980s, local artists have expressed a strong commentary on preserving the environment and on controversies focused around fishing, logging and endangered species.

The work of local photographers Jeff Wall, Rodney Graham, Fred Douglas and Marion Penner-Bancroft has earnt international renown. And sculptors Roland Brennen and Mowry Baden, using plastics, electronics and other present-day products, have set a new direction for West Coast sculpture with their kinetic creations. In addition to showing the contemporary works of resident painters, sculptors and photographers, local galleries hold regular exhibitions. These include First Nations' cedar carvings and paintings, with their traditional colourful oval designs, Inuit soapstone sculptures from the Arctic, as well as works by the Canadian Group of Seven (*www.groupofsevenart.com*) where Emily Carr was Associate Contemporary Artist, and old European and Asian masters.

*10am–5pm. Admission charge for
Conservatory. Call to verify it is open.*

University of British Columbia Botanical Garden

This showcase of plants from around
the world includes a physic garden for
medicinal herbs, planted in the
geometric design of a 16th-century
herb garden. Horticulturists here have
developed such new plants as the
Emerald Carpet, a practical, low-
spreading ground-cover plant with
little flowers. The Arbour Garden
provides cool shade where vines
abound year-round, while the Food
Garden grows fruit trees trained in
traditional styles, and the latest
vegetables. The David C Lam Asian
Garden is the largest, with 300 species
of rhododendrons, magnolias and
other species.
*6804 Southwest Marine Dr.
Tel: (604) 822 4208;
www.ubcbotanicalgarden.org.*

*Open daily, call for times.
Admission charge.*

VanDusen Botanical Garden

This 22-hectare (55-acre) mature
botanical garden with views of
Vancouver and the surrounding
mountains has gained international
recognition since its 1975 opening.
Vancouver's mild climate permits
growth and some blooms year-round.
There are more than 11,500 different
kinds of plants and 255,000 distinct
plants collected from five continents.
Gardens like the Rhododendron Walk
are planted to demonstrate botanical
relationships, or growing species in
exotic geographical areas as in the
Sino-Himalayan Garden. In between
are lakes, lawns and rock formations.
*5251 Oak St and 37th Ave, not far from
Queen Elizabeth Park. Tel: (604) 878
9274; www.vandusengarden.org. Open:
daily 10am–dusk, call to verify closing
times. Admission charge.*

VanDusen Botanical Garden

HISTORIC HOUSES

Vancouver, like Los Angeles, seems to have suffered from the philosophy of down with the old and up with the new, as far as preserving historic ('heritage') homes is concerned. But a few treasures remain.

Le Gavroche

A good way to make the past present is by enjoying a meal in a heritage home restaurant. Named after the street urchin in *Les Misérables*, Le Gavroche was established in 1979 in a refurbished three-storey Victorian house whose roof is green with moss, looking out to the Bayshore Hotel and Coal Harbour. The intimate, dimly lit interior, with its oak floors, flickering flames in the wood-burning fireplace, and dark floral-print wallpaper contrasting with white tablecloths, quickly transports diners back to a more romantic time. The restaurant is renowned for refined service, fine French cuisine and one of the city's best wine collections.
1616 Alberni St. Tel: (604) 685 3924; www.legavroche.ca

Irving House

'The handsomest, the best and most home-like house of which BC can yet boast' was the 1865 newspaper description of this 14-room home, which originally belonged to 'King of the Fraser River' Captain William Irving. The small parlour and master bedroom contain Irving's furniture, including a red rocking chair from a Fraser River sternwheeler, a piano shipped round Cape Horn in 1858 and a black horsehair settee transported across the plains from Missouri. The kitchen features a classic black and chrome pioneer stove laden with cast-iron pots and flat irons, and a hand-pumped vacuum cleaner. The kitchen floor was laid and caulked like the deck of a ship. The nursery upstairs contains a collection of dolls from the 19th century. In the library are a roll-top desk, a smoking table, a pump organ, a 17th-century grandfather clock and some fine Indian baskets.
302 Royal Ave, New Westminster. Tel: (604) 527 4640; www.nwpr.bc.ca. Open: May–Aug Wed–Sun noon–5pm; Sept–Apr noon–4pm. Admission by donation.

Roedde House

Built in 1893 by the German immigrant Gustav Roedde, Vancouver's first bookbinder, this house is part of a park site, Barclay Heritage Square, that includes nine Victorian West End houses.

Designed by F M Rattenbury, the architect responsible for the Empress Hotel, Roedde House is built in Queen Anne style, with a cupola, bay windows, an upstairs porch and a downstairs veranda. It has been furnished with period furniture to reflect city life at the turn of the 20th century.
1415 Barclay St, a ten-minute walk from the city centre. Tel: (604) 684 7040;
(Cont. on p48)

Walk: Pacific Spirit Park

A walk in the wild woods on the edge of the city offers patches of ocean framed by red cedars where squirrels scuffle through the underbrush, birds sing and serenity is all around – just a few of the pleasures of Pacific Spirit Regional Park. Personnel working on the trails are also helpful.

Allow about 2 hours, plus time for birdwatching.

Begin at Chancellor Boulevard, where the extra lane for parking begins, just beyond the Pacific Spirit Regional Park sign. Start on the Pioneer Trail, then follow the first right to the Spanish Trail, which meanders through the woods to Spanish Banks Beach or loops back on to the Pioneer Trail to the entrance.

The **Pioneer Trail** and **Spanish Trail** loop, which is about 2km (1¼ miles) long, can be muddy in sections, as is to be expected in a rainforest. The Spanish Trail heads north into tall trees and undergrowth, and for a while parallels the south edge of a tree-choked ravine. A few metres off the trail, walkers can peer down into its leafy depths.

Just a few minutes into this forest, traffic sounds fade, sunlight filters through branches overhead, and the aroma of earth and cedar fills the air. Lush ferns, salal, holly and salmonberry bushes line the trails.

Spiders' webs glisten and mushrooms cluster on fallen trunks. An occasional woodpecker drums on rotting trees, and tiny wrens and juncos flit about. A chipmunk scurries down a Douglas fir and sometimes frogs serenade. Although raccoons, weasels, skunks, otters and foxes make their homes in the undergrowth, they are usually shy when people are around.

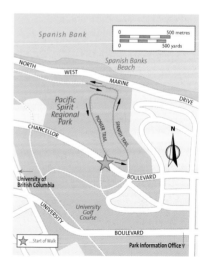

Where the trail slopes down sharply and becomes rougher, it divides. The Spanish Trail heads steeply downhill and north to Spanish Banks Beach, soon visible through the trees. The Pioneer Trail turns west, through a wooden gate.

Climb over a fallen tree trunk to an open glade called the Plains of Abraham. At the turn of the 20th century, a John Stewart ran a dairy farm here, but the once-visible foundations have now become overgrown with fireweed and blackberry bushes. A sign to the southwest indicates the Pioneer Trail, the corduroy road built by Stewart so that he could haul his milk to market.

For a longer walk, cross the western edge of the clearing and follow the winding trail north to the cliff edge, where it swings west to run parallel to the cliff tops and provides views of Burrard Inlet and the North Shore Mountains.

The trail eventually ends at a clearing on North West Marine Drive across from the beach. Blue herons spotted flying overhead are probably returning to their homes hidden in these woods.

Some 33 trails meander 53km (33 miles) through Pacific Spirit Regional Park, several beginning from the park information office. All that is needed is a map and a reasonable sense of direction. Many of the trails are popular with dog walkers, horse riders, joggers, hikers and mountain bikers. Film-makers occasionally adapt the park for sets, varying from the Amazon jungle to rural Pennsylvania.

The park is about a 20-minute drive from downtown; count on half an hour by bus (No 25). Maps (www.metrovancouver.org/about/maps/Maps/Pacificspiritmap.pdf) are available at the park information office on W 16th Avenue and at information boards at many trailheads (contact Metropolitan Vancouver Regional Parks at tel: (604) 224 5739).

Rainforest at Pacific Spirit Regional Park

The Queen Anne-style Victorian façade of Roedde House

www.roeddehouse.org. Guided tours Tue–Fri noon–4pm, Sun Tea and Tour 2–4pm. Admission charge.

Shaughnessy Walking Tour

Tree-lined and mansion-laced, the neighbourhood around South Granville makes for an interesting walking tour. The area was originally developed by the Canadian Pacific Railway as a getaway from urban life for rich Vancouverites who from 1907 on could afford homes at six times the market average. Unlike other sections of Vancouver where urban development dictated that buildings in older, outmoded architectural styles be demolished, the posh nature of Shaughnessy left many sumptuous homes alone. Tudor and neoclassical revival styles are ubiquitous in the single-family dwellings on large lots (dictated by original CPR building code requirements), in a planned suburb with curving streets and green parks. *Self-guided illustrated walking tour brochure is available online: http://vancouver.ca/commsvcs/planning/heritage/walks/w_sh_map.htm*

MUSEUMS

A wide variety of city museums provides an in-depth look at the history and cultural life of Vancouver and BC, with exhibits ranging from food and maritime history to sports and First Nations cultures.

Museum of Anthropology

A renowned Canadian museum, the Museum of Anthropology at the University of British Columbia is best known for its superb collection of art and artefacts of the province's First Nations peoples. The spectacular concrete-and-glass structure sits on a cliff overlooking English Bay and, beyond, the North Shore Mountains and Howe Sound. Inside the MOA, a dozen galleries house a great variety of objects, which express the complex social and ceremonial life of many cultures from around the world.

Entrance to the World of Art

The museum's cedar entrance doors, designed and carved by Ksan master carvers, depict the joining of heaven and earth in the creation of the first Gitxsan people. The doors, along with the adjoining side panels, form a rectangular structure inspired by the traditional Indian bent box. Carvings from traditional West Coast house interiors, with illustrations showing their original placement, border the entrance ramp. At the base of the ramp, a bear, sculpted by the late Haida artist Bill Reid, is one of the few touchable

exhibits in the museum. Be sure to feel its square snout and large teeth, nostrils and ears, characteristic of Haida bear carvings.

Great Hall

In the Great Hall, natural light streams through 15m (49ft) high windows, which illuminate an exquisite assembly of weathered cedar totem poles. Totem poles do not typically tell a story, but depict creatures representing the genealogy of the families that raised them. Ravens, bears, beavers, frogs, eagles and wolves are often an integral part of tribal crests. Totem poles have traditionally been raised to identify families or to commemorate the departed, and a raising continues to be an occasion for a potlatch, or celebration. A selection of red cedar chests, carved canoes and dishes complements the display.

Haida carvings

Vancouver

On the totem trail

At least 8,000 years ago, Asian peoples who lived by hunting and by gathering berries crossed the icy land bridge that is now the Bering Strait and drifted south along the Pacific Coast of North America and into the interior. When the Europeans arrived in the late 18th century, an estimated 80,000 of these native 'Indians' were living in what is now known as BC. Within a century, however, two-thirds of them had died from imported diseases.

Today, there are more than 130,000 people of census-identified aboriginal North American Indian ancestry living in BC. The Salish inhabit the southwest of the province (the Lower Mainland) and the southeastern part of Vancouver Island. On the west coast of Vancouver Island are the Nootka. Further north along the coast reside the Kwakiutl, Bella Coola, Tsimshian, Haida and Tlingit peoples. Between 1973 and 2010, treaty negotiations settled 22 native land

The exquisite artistry of the Northwest Coast Indian totem poles in Vancouver's Stanley Park

Totem poles are heavy with symbolism

claims across Canada, and more are under negotiation. The struggle to regain self-esteem and self-reliance has accelerated, including the renaming of the Queen Charlotte Islands, traditional lands of the Haida Nation, Haida Gwaii, in December 2009. There has been a visible renaissance in the arts, in totem poles, masks, talking sticks, bent boxes, canoes, clothing and jewellery.

Totem poles, the largest woodcarvings known, are scattered throughout Vancouver, with other fine examples elsewhere in BC: Victoria's Thunderbird Park and Royal BC Museum; Duncan on Vancouver Island; and in Haida Gwaii's heritage sites. Some of Vancouver's best are in Stanley Park, at the Museum of Anthropology (*see p49*) and at the Capilano Suspension Bridge (*see pp80 & 155*). Some of these carved cedar poles are memorials to the dead, others portray family trees, while still others relate mythological adventures.

Carved in a stylised realism, totem poles are sometimes difficult to decipher. Here are some commonly seen creatures. The thunderbird is the creator and controller of all elements and spirits. The raven is credited with providing light, fire and water. The whale symbolises strength and bravery. The bear, regarded as an elder kinsman, represents strength, authority and mobility. The eagle depicts wisdom, authority and power, and the salmon enriches with abundance and prosperity.

Highlights of the galleries

Look for intricately carved miniatures in silver, gold, argillite, ivory, bone, horn and wood, mostly dating from the 19th century.

The highlight of the contemporary collection is the acclaimed sculpture *The Raven and the First Men*, carved in laminated yellow cedar by Bill Reid, and displayed in a skylighted rotunda. The sculpture is a dramatic portrayal of the birth of mankind, with the first Haida people emerging both frontwards and backwards from a partially open clam shell (*see p42*) – you'll see it on the Canadian $20 note.

Behind this sculpture, several cases display 30 of Reid's smaller carvings in cedar, boxwood and argillite, along with some gold and silver jewellery pieces. These works span 40 years of creative activity, from early explorations in Haida design to his distinctive, mature style, now recognised around the world.

The Research Collections, since the museum is both a public and a teaching institution, feature a visible storage system, with a series of glass-covered drawers and cases that let visitors see but not touch more than 10,000 objects, arranged in cultural and artefact categories. The Audain Gallery presents changing shows of MOA and international cultural arts objects.

The outdoor exhibits

One of the best exhibits is outdoors on the grassy area between the museum and the cliff. The Kwakiutl, Haida and Gitxsan totem poles standing here with two Haida houses, one for the living and one for the dead, are completely at one with nature. Two carved house posts are by artists of Musqueam

The Museum of Anthropology displays a fine collection of Northwest Coast Indian art

heritage, the First Nations people that inhabited the land here.

On the UBC campus at 6393 North West Marine Dr. Tel: (604) 822 5087; www.moa.ubc.ca. Open: summer Tue 10am–9pm, Wed–Mon 10am–5pm; winter Tue 10am–9pm, Wed–Sun 10am–5pm. Admission charge, reduced Tue evenings.

BC Golf Museum and Hall of Fame

A collection of golf memorabilia to delight the enthusiastic golfer.

2545 Blanca St. Tel: (604) 222 4653; http://bcgolfhouse.com. Call for open dates and times.

BC Sports Hall of Fame and Museum

This museum provides high-tech, hands-on sports entertainment. Visitors can run, throw, climb and row their way through the computer-enhanced Hall of Champions, which honours BC's elite athletes and teams, or test their athletic skills against top competitors in the Participation Gallery. The museum covers 150 years of history, from 1850s native games to videos of recent sporting events.

At BC Place Stadium. Tel: (604) 647 7414; www.bcsportshalloffame.com. Closed for facility renovation until 2011.

Canadian Museum of Flight

This outdoor assembly of vintage aircraft includes bombers, biplanes, jets and helicopters. The museum

CAPTAIN GEORGE VANCOUVER

George Vancouver, an English youth of Dutch descent, joined the British navy at the age of 13, and went on to serve Captain Cook on his second and third voyages. In 1791, Captain Vancouver set out from England aboard HMS *Discovery*, sailed south around the Cape of Good Hope, and a year later reached the northern Pacific Coast of North America. He had been tasked to survey the coast and negotiate a land settlement with Spanish Captain Bodega y Quadra, at Nootka, on what is now known as Vancouver Island.

Without realising that the Spaniards had charted this region before him, Vancouver claimed all the land he saw for King George III.

Vancouver returned to England in 1795 and died three years later aged 40. Spain, after the Mexican Revolution, eventually abandoned all claims to the Pacific northwest.

also has a picnic area and playground.

Hangar 3, 5333-216 St, Langley. Tel: (604) 532 0035; www.canadianflight. org. Open: summer daily 10am–5pm; winter 10am–4pm. Admission charge.

H R MacMillan Space Centre

Multimedia Planetarium Star Theatre astronomy shows, including special shows for children, and Canada's best laser and light show on Friday and Saturday nights, beamed on to a 20m (66ft) dome, bring the cosmos within reach. The cosmic interactive gallery puts visitors at the controls. There is also a variety of special presentations in the GroundStation Canada mission control theatre, and exciting simulated journeys through space. The centre also

Crab sculpture at the H R MacMillan Space Centre

has some authentic space artefacts to see and a real moon rock to touch.
1100 Chestnut St, Vanier Park.
Tel: (604) 738 7827; www.spacecentre.ca.
Open: Jul–Aug daily 10am–5pm;
Sept–Jun Mon–Fri 10am–3pm, Sat,
Sun & holidays 10am–5pm.
Admission charge.

Museum of Vancouver

This museum, housing one of the largest civic collections in Canada, is devoted to regional history and the First Nations, but also features exhibitions of decorative arts from all over the world.
1100 Chestnut St. Tel: (604) 736 4431;
www.museumofvancouver.ca. Open:
Jul–Aug Thur 10am–8pm, Fri–Wed
10am–5pm; Sept–Jun Tue, Wed &
Fri–Sun 10am–5pm, Thur 10am–8pm.
Admission charge.

Vancouver Maritime Museum

This Vanier Park museum explores the maritime world, with exciting tales of the sea and hands-on activities in its Children's Maritime Discovery Centre. There is a huge collection of model ships and many special exhibitions. The museum is home to the *St Roch*, a two-masted schooner which is now a National Historic Site (*see p12*). Built in the 1920s, it became the first ship to navigate through the treacherous waters of the Northwest Passage. The many 360-degree online virtual tours preview museum exhibits and highlights such as viewing the *St Roch* from her foremast.
1905 Ogden Ave. Tel: (604) 257 8300;
www.vancouvermaritimemuseum.com.
Open: summer daily 10am–5pm; winter
Tue–Sat 10am–5pm, Sun noon–5pm.
Admission charge.

THE ORPHEUM: A CANADIAN CLASSIC

Here, in one of North America's youngest cities, the past is wonderfully preserved in the Orpheum theatre. This gracious old building has hosted such great artists as Charlie Chaplin, Igor Stravinsky and Helen Hayes. Its grand opening in 1927 was a social highlight. With 2,800 seats, it was then the largest theatre on the Pacific Coast. The premiere featured a silent movie, but people really came to see the vaudeville, featuring everybody's favourite: Toto the clown with his little dog, Whiskey.

Interior and backstage wonders

The Orpheum has always been a star, even with mediocre performers. Originally built as a link in the Chicago-based theatre chain, it was designed in Spanish Renaissance/Baroque or Moorish style, with a basic colour scheme of antique ivory and gold. Ornamented pilasters and colonnades, highlighted with imitation and sometimes real gold leaf, contrasted with rich tapestries of black and gold arabesques, creating an aura of exotic luxury. Dramatic maroon velvet draperies lent a regal touch. A hundred glittering chandeliers lit the hall.

Beneath the stage, an electrically operated mechanism raised and lowered three big Wurlitzer organs, which sounded like a full orchestra. One is still played a few times every year. An animal room accommodated

VANC...
O...

The historic Orpheu... to the Vancouver Symph... 1930. Each year, apart from a... season extending from October t... orchestra presents special outdoor c... around the region in summer. In Septem... 2000, Bramwell Tovey became Music Director. Also gifted as an orator, Tovey gives regular lectures on forthcoming programmes an hour before the performance starts – arrive an hour early in order to avail yourself of this opportunity.

601 Smythe St. Tel: (604) 876 3434 (information and customer service for ticket purchase); www.vancouversymphony.ca

the dogs, monkeys, tigers and elephants featured in some of the shows. An efficient ventilation system changed the air every three minutes. One Orpheum manager said the downstairs was uncomfortably reminiscent of *The Phantom of the Opera*.

Famous Players and the talkies

During the early 1930s, when live music faded and talking pictures took over, the Orpheum passed into the hands of Famous Players Theatres. The Nabob Company sponsored elegant afternoon teas on the mezzanine. One of the Orpheum's proudest moments was the Canadian premiere of *Gone with the Wind* in 1939. The theatre has attracted countless famous faces, including Marilyn Monroe, who came in 1956 to publicise *Gentlemen Prefer Blondes*.

(*Cont. on p58*)

VANCOUVER SYMPHONY ORCHESTRA

theatre has been home
ny Orchestra since
full orchestra

o April, the
concerts
ber

Vancouver

55

anville Island

is actually a peninsula. Once a swampy,
er the industrial heart of Vancouver, these
acres) of land are now an urban oasis of
s and renovated warehouses, popular for
ps and galleries, restaurants and other
ed here (see www.granvilleisland.com).

hours, plus extra time for more leisurely
a meal.

Walk south from downtown for ten minutes to the foot of Hornby St and take the five-minute Aquabus (www.theaquabus.com) mini-ferry ride across False Creek, or board False Creek Ferries (www.granvilleislandferries.bc.ca) at the Aquatic Centre and other stops to go across. There is complimentary one- or three-hour parking for cars and three hours for boats on the island, but places and dock spaces are extremely hard to find. It is much better to go on foot.

1 From the Aquabus ferry

Leaving the Aquabus ferry, veer to the left of the Public Market through the courtyard area, walking by the Arts Club Theatre to cross to the island information centre. Don't resist the Public Market, well worth a stroll through, to enjoy the aroma of a great array of local and imported food, from baked breads to seafood, local fruit and green vegetables, and artisan crafts. Edible BC (*www.edible-britishcolumbia.com*) conducts Chef Guided Market

Experiences Tours, popular with visitors and Vancouverites. On the waterfront, a bevy of buskers, including clowns and jugglers, entertain benches of visitors.

Northwest of the market is a good place to watch the yachts and motor-boats slip out to English Bay beyond. The deck at Bridges Restaurant (there may be a queue) is a super spot to sit in the sun or watch the sunset.
Turn south into Duranleau St.

2 Duranleau Street

Maritime Market, in several buildings along Duranleau Street, sports a series of maritime shops selling rugged outdoor wear, scuba gear, yacht fittings and other nautical equipment. Across the street, the Net Loft shelters a dozen shops, including Edie Hats with a selection of stylish headgear; The Postcard Place; Paper Ya, which features handmade paper from around the world; glass and pottery studios; and the Wickaninnish Gallery of native jewellery and sculptures.
Cross Anderson St.

3 Granville Island Brewing

Across Anderson Street, the brewery produces a popular preservative-free light lager (Bavarian-style Pilsner) and other types of beer, with tours and tastings every afternoon.
Cross over to Cartwright St.

4 Cartwright Street

The Kids Market (*www.kidsmarket.ca*) houses 28 shops and other activity areas. East of the Waterfront Theatre and the Cats Social House restaurant is the supervised Water Park. The rest of Cartwright Street is lined with art studios, galleries and craft shops.
Continue east to the Granville Island Hotel and the Sea Village.

5 Sea Village

On the north shore, near a big, rusting crane overhead, is a fleet of floating homes, many with skylights and patios

crowded with plants and flowers. Walk partway down the ramp to see a colourful collection of rural mailboxes.
Walk northwest along the boardwalk to the Emily Carr University of Art & Design.

6 Emily Carr University of Art & Design

Here, big windows reveal students at work. Visitors are welcome to view the student art exhibits in the foyer. Beyond a few more craft shops along the shore is the ferry dock.

Visitors can sign up for classes at the art studios, catch live music in the Public Market Courtyard, or learn to sail on nearby English Bay. You can also rent a kayak to paddle up False Creek.
Return to the ferry.

Walk: Granville Island

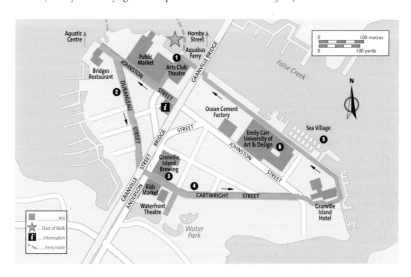

Inside the Orpheum

Snack-vending machines appeared in the Orpheum in 1942, and a confectionery counter in 1945. By 1950, usherettes were selling confections from trays in the auditorium. From 1943 to 1954, Nabob's Harmony House was broadcast from coast to coast from 'Canada's most beautiful theatre'. One of the last grand premieres was *King Rat* in 1965, with a guest appearance by author James Clavell, then living in West Vancouver.

The Vancouver Symphony Orchestra has been a frequent performer here since the early 1930s.

Restoration to former glory

In 1973, Famous Players Theatres announced that the Orpheum would be gutted to create six mini-cinemas, reflecting a continuing trend towards smaller theatres. Vancouverites wrote 8,500 letters in protest. Consequently, the city purchased the Orpheum for $3.9 million, and spent almost as much restoring the acoustics and fine furnishings. Octogenarian artist and decorator Tony Heinsbergen, who had worked on the original structure in 1927, supervised the interior decoration and painted the *Orpheus* mural on the massive 18m (60ft) dome. Florentine Joseph Tinucci did much of the ornate and decorative plasterwork, and reproduced the columns that are now part of the soundshell.

In 1977, the Orpheum reopened, the finest heritage concert hall in the country. In 1983, a new foyer was completed, and the Orpheum was declared a National Historic Site. Acoustics were improved in 1995 and it was again refurbished in 2009. The Orpheum is home to Vancouver's Symphony Orchestra, Bach Choir, Chamber Choir and Cantata Singers, and the BC Entertainment Hall of Fame with its lobby staircase Starwall photo gallery.

884 Granville, Smythe and Seymour Sts. Tel: (604) 665 3050; http://vancouver.ca/ commsvcs/cultural/theatres. Guided tours on request (charge).

PLACES OF WORSHIP

There are dozens of places of worship in Vancouver, thanks to the variety of visitors from all over the world who have settled here. The following are a few that might be of interest to anyone, regardless of creed. A listing of churches is found in the Practical Guide section on *p184*.

Buddhist Temple

This temple is an exquisite example of Chinese palatial architecture, with gilded porcelain tiles and flying rooftop dragons. The interior is an artistic showcase of classic Chinese sculpture, painting and murals, and of inscriptions, carpentry and embroidery. An outdoor courtyard encloses a beautiful collection of bonsai plants and a ceramic mural of Kuan-Yin-Bodhisattva.

A 30-minute drive south from downtown; turn west at the exit by Fantasy Gardens towards Steveston. 9160 Steveston Highway, Richmond. Tel: (604) 274 2822; www.buddhisttemple. ca. Open: daily 9.30am–5.30pm. Free admission.

Canadian Memorial Church

Shortly after World War I, Chaplain George Fallis came to Vancouver with the idea of building a memorial to Canadians who had served in the war. He found a congregation with the same idea, solicited the support of local leaders, and then headed east across

A corner of the garden at the Buddhist Temple

Vancouver

Canada to find further funding. The result was the Canadian Memorial Church, which opened in 1928 at the 11th hour of the 11th day of the 11th month – mortgage-free.

The church is constructed in grey stone, Gothic-style. The main attraction is the stained-glass windows, each of which depicts a biblical scene. The provincial coats of arms beneath are flanked by historical illustrations.

The BC window depicts a soldier's faith, with Christ meeting a Roman centurion pleading on behalf of his palsied servant. The historical panels show Captain Vancouver at Nootka Sound in 1792 and Simon Fraser exploring the Fraser River in 1808.

The Nova Scotia window illustrates the arrival of Jacques Cartier in 1543 and of Lord Rollo, the first Englishman, in 1759. The Yukon window depicts the Chilkoot Pass in 1898 and a Royal Mail dog team with carriole.

The spectacular chancel window portrays a biblical motif of sacrifice and young manhood. The all-Canada window facing north depicts the services rendered by all men and women of Canada throughout World War I.

The windows are interesting for their comments on world peace and history and for their exquisite craftsmanship. *1825 W 16th Ave at the southwest corner of Burrard St. Tel: (604) 731 3101; www.canadianmemorial.org. Open: regular church services are held on Sun morning at 10.30am, but for many visitors who may prefer to study the windows in relative solitude, staff at the community centre, adjacent to the church on 16th Ave, keep the keys and escort those interested to the chapel during regular business hours.*

Christ Church Anglican Cathedral

Located in the heart of downtown Vancouver, this century-old sanctuary looks as though it should be nestled into a green valley in rural England. Of special interest are the English and Canadian stained-glass windows, and a tableau of the Crucifixion. *690 Burrard St. Tel: (604) 682 3848; www.cathedral.vancouver.bc.ca. Open: Mon–Fri 9.30am–4pm. Free admission.*

Westminster Abbey

This modern Benedictine monastery is both a high school and a degree-granting theological seminary. Every Sunday the ten bells of the 50m (164ft) tower chime over the valley to announce mass. Resident monks create and restore paintings and other forms of art in an atmosphere of peace and tranquillity. Various sculptures, stained-glass windows and murals decorate the monastery. Overnight rooms are available (reservations recommended), as St Benedict believed that there should always be guests at a monastery. *34224 Dewdney Trunk Rd, near the town of Mission, an hour's drive east from Vancouver. Tel: (604) 826 8975. Open: Mon–Fri 1.30–4pm, Sun 2–4pm. Guided tours available. Modest dress requested. Donations accepted.*

SCIENCE WORLD AT TELUS WORLD OF SCIENCE

A hundred years ago, the site of Science World was a watery swamp. Today, its silver geodesic sphere is a city landmark. Billed as the most curious place on earth, this science complex attracts 525,000 enquiring minds a year, with 750,000 anticipated after Science World's facility and site refurbishment is complete in 2011. Expect expanded gallery space; some areas described below may be renamed. Science World remains open during construction. Most visitors like to spend several hours at Science World, and many enjoy lunch or a snack before moving on.

Scientific wonders discovered

Our World focuses on the challenges and solutions of creating a sustainable future. The exhibit addresses real-world issues including sustainability, electricity, water consumption, wind power and solar energy.

In the Eureka! Gallery on the second level, visitors can learn about everything from potential energy to sound through bright, engaging exhibits and games. The nearby Search Sarah Stern Gallery focuses on the natural history of BC and elsewhere. There are tree roots hanging from the ceiling, a crawl-through beaver lodge, a hollow red cedar tree and a see-through beehive.

Bodyworks offers interactive exhibits that investigate individual strength, endurance, speed, reaction time, dexterity, ac... more. The ... performan... between a... are one f...

In the... interacti... regular... challenging puzzles (Chinese puzzles which consist of several basic shapes which can be combined to form a great variety of other figures) and geometric shapes; and the study of physiognomy, in which the curious can observe how faces express feeling, deceive, encode identity and record experiences.

1455 Quebec St, a...
St/Science Wor...
Tel: (604) 4...
www.scie...
62
Vancouver

Big-screen excitement

The third level houses the 400-seat OMNIMAX® Theatre (the screen is 27m/89ft wide), where the audience is surrounded with awesome larger-than-life images on one of the world's largest domed screens and engulfed in wrap-around sound.

Dazzling demonstrations

Science World presents audience participation shows daily at Centre Stage. These lively and entertaining programmes focus on such diverse subjects as bubbles, balance, kinetic engineering and liquid nitrogen. Designed to keep youngsters in touch with the very latest discoveries in science and technology, Science World organises special events for children from time to time.

cross from the Main
SkyTrain station.
3 7443;
ceworld.ca.

Open: Mon–Fri 10am–5pm, Sat & Sun
10am–6pm. Admission charge.
The Aquabus and False Creek Ferries
stop here.

The futuristic Science World is a spectacular city landmark

STANLEY PARK

In a province as vast and varied as BC, there are many close-to-nature hideaways. But it is relatively rare to find an urban wilderness so accessible to so many people. About a ten-minute walk from downtown, the park covers an area of 400 hectares (988 acres, about the same size as Central Park in New York City), jutting northwards into Burrard Inlet and marking the entrance to Vancouver Harbour. Surrounding it is a 8.8km (5½-mile) section of Vancouver's sea wall, popular with walkers, cyclists and rollerbladers.

From wilderness to park

Remarkable foresight on the part of Vancouver's city council in 1886 resulted in the creation of Stanley Park. The swampy peninsula was then a naval reserve where deer, bear, raccoon and cougar roamed along narrow trails and abandoned logging roads. The council petitioned the federal government to set it aside as a park.

The petition was granted, leaving only Deadman's Island as a naval base. So a year after it opened in 1888, Lord Stanley, Governor-General of Canada, dedicated the park 'to the use and enjoyment of people of all colours, creeds and customs for all time'.

A park for all tastes

Today, about 8 million people a year come from all over Canada and the world to enjoy Stanley Park. Even on a warm summer day, visitors who do not want to mingle with the crowds can seek out the solitude of a shady trail.

Stanley Park is many things to many people. To youngsters, it is the sandy beach, a baby beluga whale, or a miniature railway. To teenagers, it is a trysting place and a playground for such sports as football (soccer), skateboarding, rollerblading and cycling.

To families, the park often means a leisurely Sunday picnic on a blanket under weeping willows. To the many elderly who live nearby in the West End concrete jungle, this urban oasis provides access to nature and the opportunity for a pleasant stroll around Lost Lagoon to feed the birds and squirrels.

Recovery and restoration

This once densely forested park was hit by a devastating storm in December 2006. An estimated 10,000 trees were lost, many blown over by high winds, and popular trails became unusable. The city commenced restoration and reforestation of the park, reinforced and rebuilt sea walls, repaired roads and trails, and encouraged environmental art projects.

Park wildlife

After the windstorm in 2006, the Stanley Park Ecology Society (*see www.stanleyparkecology.ca*) undertook a study to identify species living in or no longer seen in the park. It found 30 species of mammals, but no large mammals; 236 bird species, including a

Vancouver

The Teahouse, Stanley Park

blue heron colony near the Society Centre at Nature House; a small number of amphibians and reptiles, and 72 types of fish.

There are few wild animals in the park today, except for the sea life in the aquarium, and the squirrels, raccoons and skunks around Lost Lagoon. Occasionally, a black-tailed deer swims over from the North Shore. The last cougar disappeared nearly 50 years ago.

Lost Lagoon and Beaver Lake are wetlands, attractive to migratory birds and permanent residents. The beavers were removed from Beaver Lake years ago, because their efficient sawmill and logging operations were destroying many trees and leaving others to fall on unsuspecting visitors. They also dug tunnels that undermined the miniature railway and penetrated the bison pen.

Migratory birds introduced carp to the Lost Lagoon, so named by poetess Pauline Johnson because its waters used to disappear at low tide. The water, now locked in by man-made devices, is fresh.

Lost Lagoon bird sanctuary is home to cormorants, mergansers, scaups, ringbills, green wing-tails, shovelers, mallard and many other species, including bald eagles, which have several nests in the park. Look for the herons' return in February. A few hundred Canada geese are permanent residents; another thousand or so fly in for the winter. In spring, mother geese, ducks and swans parade around with gaggles of young ones.

VANCOUVER HARBOUR

Vancouver Harbour is Canada's largest port and one of the busiest in the world – the country's gateway to the Pacific Rim – and it plays a key role in international trade. Every year about 3,000 ships, most flying foreign flags, carry bulk, general and containerised cargo between Vancouver and a hundred other ports around the world. The terminals circling Vancouver Harbour move more than 102 million tonnes of cargo annually. For more information visit *www.portmetrovancouver.com*

Beyond the Inner Harbour east of Second Narrows Bridge are several oil refineries and a major sulphur export operation at Port Moody. About 35km (22 miles) south of downtown, near the BC Ferries dock at Tsawwassen, the Westshore Terminals at Roberts Bank in Delta ship coal to other countries.

Canada Place Promenade

Canada Place Pier is a wraparound public promenade for observing the Inner Harbour. The 'Canadian Trail' along the pier promenade uses tiles and coloured glass to show Canada's provinces and territories. A nightly 'Sails of Light' on Canada Place's five sails colours them with images and animation. A high-definition billboard-sized video screen featuring more Canada images is over the front of Canada Place. Luxurious cruise ships depart to Alaska from the Cruise Terminal here from May to September. For more information, check *www.canadaplace.ca*

Panoramic vantage points

Harbour-view rooms at the Pan Pacific, The Fairmont Waterfront and Renaissance Vancouver Harbourside hotels enable visitors to Vancouver to get oriented quickly. Vancouver Lookout (*555 West Hastings St; tel: (604) 689 0421; www. vancouverlookout.com*), a circular observation deck, affords a 360-degree view of the harbour and the city, and plaques and decorative display panels relate the history and character of the area.

Views from the water

For a view of the harbour from the water, take the 12-minute SeaBus (*www.translink.ca*) passenger ferry from the downtown Waterfront Terminal to North Vancouver. Alternatively, contact the Tourism Vancouver Visitor Centre (*tel: (604) 683 2000; www. tourismvancouver.com*) for details about harbour cruises.

Waterfront parks

Several parks around Burrard Inlet offer great picnic spots and harbour views. From the **Stanley Park Port of Vancouver Viewpoint**, on the sea wall just south of Brockton Point, almost the whole harbour is visible. A series of plaques outlines port operations.

Much smaller **Portside Park**, just east of Canada Place at the foot of Main Street, offers grassy slopes, children's play areas and a good view of various

(*Cont. on p70*)

Vancouver

Stanley Park attractions

Shortly after the park opened in 1888, the warden adopted a black bear, which he kept tethered to a tree. The local vicar's wife used to bring over household scraps to feed the bear, but one day he ignored the food and took a swipe at the lady's skirt. He was banished to a bear pit, and it was decided to set aside an enclosed section of the park for wild animals.

The zoo grew to house 400 animals representing 90 different species. However, it was shut down because people were concerned about the relatively small area the animals had to live in. All that remains is the **Children's Farmyard**. As well as the usual rabbits and goats, this petting zoo includes such unusual species as Jacob sheep, Vietnamese pot-bellied

White beluga whales never fail to draw attention at the Vancouver Aquarium

pigs, alpacas and a llama. To see wild animals, visitors must now drive an hour east from downtown to the Greater Vancouver Zoo (*tel: (604) 856 6825; www.gvzoo.com*) in Aldergrove, where giraffes, lions, tigers, camels, hippos and 100 other species roam a rangeland.

The Stanley Park Miniature Railway has always carried more adults than children. Passengers ride in little canopied coaches, sometimes pulled by a replica of the Canadian Pacific Railway engine No 374, which brought the first transcontinental train in to Vancouver in 1887. The ten-minute ride along the 20in narrow-gauge rails goes through an avalanche tunnel and round a small artificial lake.
Tel: (604) 257 8531. Open: Jul–early Sept daily 10.30am–5pm; rest of the year Sat, Sun & special events 11am–4pm, depending on weather. Call in advance. Admission charge.

Vancouver Aquarium

The Vancouver Aquarium is home to more than 70,000 creatures, including 33,700 fish; 30,000 invertebrates such as jellyfish and octopuses; reptiles, amphibians, birds and more. A 5.5m

(18ft) high bronze sculpture of a leaping killer whale, *Chief of the Undersea World*, expertly crafted by Haida artist Bill Reid, marks the entrance.

Inside the aquarium, the more active denizens of the deep range from delicate sea horses to crocodiles. The Marine Mammal Deck is a great viewing place. A wall-sized viewing window shows playful sea otters cavorting above and below water. On the same deck is another area for harbour seals.

The Arctic Canada exhibition lets visitors look beneath the polar ice of the High Arctic at graceful white beluga whales; the big underwater windows make for excellent viewing.

The Treasures of the BC Coast Gallery displays such Canadian coastal water residents as giant octopuses, silvery salmon and waving sea anemones. The Wild Coast walkways have great viewing of sea otters, Steller sea lions, harbour seals, Pacific white-sided dolphins, and their trainers feeding them and working with the dolphins and sea lions. Special extra-charge animal encounter programmes allow visitors to work with beluga whales, dolphins, sea lions, sea otters and sea turtles.

The humid Amazon Rainforest Gallery pathways wind through a tropical jungle, with banana and other equatorial trees where sloths

A statue of the orca killer whale, no longer seen live at the Vancouver Aquarium

hang lazily in the heat. Brightly coloured tropical birds – and in summer, butterflies – flit among tiny treetop marmosets, while in the water reside anacondas, piranhas, stingrays and electric eels.

The Tropical Zone features steely-eyed sharks, fed twice a week, and rainbows of reef fishes. Children under eight years old enjoy the Clowfish Cove tidal pools, where they can touch anemones, chitons and starfish. There are daily Dive Shows and Meet the Trainer talks.
Stanley Park Aquarium.
Tel: (604) 659 3521;
www.visitvanaqua.org,
www.vanaqua.org. Open: summer daily 9.30am–7pm; winter daily 9.30am–5pm. Admission charge.

By bike: The sea wall

The Stanley Park Seawall, one of the best urban cycle routes in the world, is the middle section of the 22km (14-mile) sea wall from Burrard Inlet to Kitsilano Beach. Near the park's Georgia St entrance, ten-minutes' walk from most downtown hotels, bicycles and tandems can be hired by the hour.

Allow about 2 hours.

The 8.8km (5½-mile) long paved pathway follows the perimeter of the 400-hectare (988-acre) peninsular park. The right side (inside) of the pathway, which is mostly level, is for cyclists and rollerbladers, runs anticlockwise, and begins at Lost Lagoon. Walk bikes along the underpass and right to the sea wall.

1 Vancouver Rowing Club

Just past the Km 0 sign is the Tudor-style Vancouver Rowing Club. Single sculls and eights skim Coal Harbour's sheltered waters. Across the harbour, the city skyline is highlighted by the big white canvas sails of Canada Place. Almost opposite the rowing club stands a statue of Lord Stanley, a former Governor-General of Canada who, in 1889, dedicated the park 'to the use and enjoyment of people of all colours, creeds and customs for all time'.

2 Nine O'Clock Gun

A little further along stands a statue of Scottish poet Robert Burns and another of Harry Jerome, once the world's fastest runner. The Nine O'Clock Gun, which once called herring fishermen home, still booms every evening.

3 Brockton Point

A bright red-and-white-striped lighthouse marks Brockton Point. Across Burrard Inlet brilliant yellow piles of sulphur await export. Behind lies Brockton Oval, a cinder jogging track encircling a cricket pitch which is used by rugby players in winter. A little further along stands the bronze sculpture of *Girl in a Wet Suit*.

4 Lumberman's Arch

At Lumberman's Arch, near Km 3, grassy slopes overlook the children's water park. Once the site of a Squamish native village, tons of seashells from the midden were used to surface the first road in the park in 1888. It is a short cycle off the sea wall to the Vancouver Aquarium and Children's Farmyard (*see pp66–7*).

5 Prospect Point

Prospect Point is the park's highest point. A cairn commemorates the SS *Beaver*, the steamship that sank nearby in 1888. View the huge pillars that support the Lions Gate Bridge.

6 Siwash Rock

A little further on is Siwash Rock, the subject of an Indian legend. Millennia ago, a young chief and his wife lived nearby. When their son was born the chief plunged into the waters to cleanse himself and so ensure a spotless life for the newborn. At that moment giants in a canoe demanded that the chief go ashore. He refused, and they were so impressed by his love and devotion to the child that they transformed him into Siwash Rock, to stand forever as a monument to clean fatherhood. The legend was recorded a century ago by First Nations poetess Pauline Johnson, who is buried in a leafy glade nearby.

7 Second Beach

Second Beach has a popular children's playground and a sandy beach. The cycle trail crosses the main road through the park, and passes a Japanese-style bridge crossing a willow-banked stream. Beyond are a pitch-and-putt golf course, putting green, tennis courts and The Fish House restaurant. *The trail continues over a humped bridge and follows the southern shore along Lost Lagoon to loop back to the start of the tour.*

By bike: The sea wall

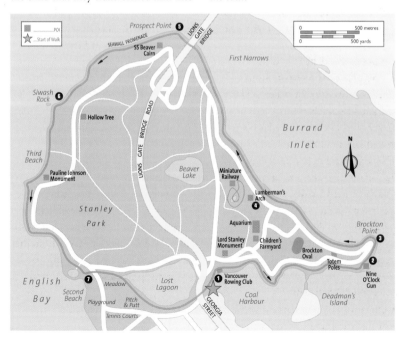

marine activities. Further east, **New Brighton Park**, just off McGill Street and west of the Second Narrows Bridge, has a pool, a pier, lots of open space, views of Cascadia Terminals grain elevators and of ships sailing through the Second Narrows.

Waterfront Park, located between the Lonsdale Quay (SeaBus Terminal) and the Pacific Marine Training Institute in North Vancouver, provides a panorama of the harbour and the city skyline. **Harbour View Park**, located further east on a narrow strip of land at the mouth of North Vancouver's

Lynn Creek, features a creek-side walking trail and a platform for observing the loading and unloading of forest products.

YALETOWN

Yaletown, the trendiest downtown area, centres around Mainland Street between Nelson and Davie Streets. Just over a century ago, this neighbourhood was rainforest wilderness – until 1887, when the Canadian Pacific Railway moved its operations from the little town of Yale to this spot on the north shore of False Creek. A shanty town of

Brockton Point Lighthouse stands at the east end of Stanley Park

A street in trendy Yaletown

wood-frame homes, boarding houses and hotels developed here. One of the wooden homes from 1907 still stands at 1021 Richards Street.

From the early 20th century, brick warehouses replaced the wooden structures. By the 1950s, most residents had moved to the suburbs. In recent years, creative people have been converting the old warehouses into work and retail space, resulting in wonderful walking streets lined with shops, galleries and restaurants.

The growing selection of stores specialises in art supplies, coffee, flowers, designer and discounted clothing, sports and legal attire, and pricey home furnishings.

The Yaletown Galleria, at 1080 Mainland, houses three floors of offices and shops overlooking a central atrium. It's home to showrooms for antiques, furniture and accessories ranging from oriental urns to the latest in interior modern design. Drop in to Design House at 1110 Mainland Street to see how chic Vancouverites are furnishing their flats, or Global Atomic Designs at 1006 Mainland for the latest in street fashion.

Chic condos are sprouting around Yaletown's perimeter. It is the kind of place where the Business Improvement Association talks about the 'patio scene', referring to oversize outdoor patio dining areas, many of brick, the former warehouse loading docks where building at the same level as the lorry bed meant fewer bad backs for workers. The chic and those searching for a good time and party atmosphere find the district, northeast of Granville Island, their Soho. For more information *see www.yaletowninfo.com*

Harbour life

Vancouver is the largest port in Canada, providing the vital link with the Pacific Rim nations. It will come as no surprise, therefore, to discover that Vancouver Harbour was once almost exclusively industrial. This is no longer the case. Extensive development is underway, concentrated in three main areas, all of which are on the waterfront: Coal Harbour, near Stanley Park; Yaletown, where redevelopment is complete; and East False Creek, near the Science World.

The development at Coal Harbour is one of the most extensive waterfront revitalisations in North America. Stretching east of Stanley Park to the Vancouver Convention Centre at the foot of Burrard Street, Coal Harbour comprises a marina, park, community centre, offices and retail development. A number of town houses and residential towers offer upmarket living, a short ten-minute walk from downtown Vancouver.

The skyline forms a stunning backdrop to harbour life

Vancouver is a busy port

towers – spurred on by the development of the Olympic/Paralympic Village on False Creek near Science World, completes the revitalisation of this erstwhile neglected harbour area.

The pace of life in that part of the harbour occupied by pleasure craft is gentle. One resident, who has worked aboard his floating electronic cottage/houseboat for 20 years, says the tides are for him the pulse of Mother Nature. If he were never to leave his home for a whole year, he would still travel over 5km (3 miles), since harbour tides advance and retreat as much as 4.5m (15ft) twice daily.

Canada geese paddle up to his houseboat most mornings for breakfast, while hunched blue herons stalk along the shore for snacks, and kingfishers dive for minnows. Loons and cormorants patrol the waters, along with ever-present shrieking seagulls. Starfish and mussels hug the pillars that keep the docks in place, while crabs crawl and feed along the bottom. Harbour seals occasionally watch from further offshore.

In winter, harbour-dwellers can pull out binoculars and look up to Grouse Mountain across Burrard Inlet to see if there's still room for more skiers on the slopes. It's quite a lifestyle!

In the 1980s Yaletown was the industrial backyard of downtown Vancouver, full of warehouses and light industry – it even had a sawmill. Today, while the distinctive stone-paved streets and many stone and brick buildings still remain, the warehouses have been replaced by trendy furniture showrooms, boutique shops and design studios. The streets are dotted with fashionable restaurants, nightclubs and coffee houses. Residential development in this now upmarket and popular area hugs the waterfront.

The redevelopment along East and Southeast False Creek – clusters of

Tour: Boat ride on a bus

The SeaBus provides an inexpensive harbour cruise, along with a great opportunity to explore Lonsdale Quay and Waterfront Park in North Vancouver. The crossing takes 12 minutes.

Allow 2 hours.

Start the tour at the Waterfront Station, at the end of Water St.

1 SeaBus Terminal

Tall, creamy pillars mark the entrance to this classic old brick building. The beautifully renovated interior of the terminal showcases a series of paintings from 1916 of the Rocky Mountains, looking down on a large lobby near shops, fast-food stops and coffee bars. *Pause on the overhead ramp to the SeaBus to watch railcars being shunted over the shining rails, as trains load and unload. Then board the SeaBus for the sail across the Inner Harbour.*

The SeaBuses have no outside decks, but the windows provide a maritime artwork of freighters with many foreign flags, luxury cruise ships sailing to and from Alaska, a variety of smaller pleasure craft, and float planes taking off and landing. North looms the imposing majesty of the Coast Range, west the forest-green peninsula of Stanley Park, and the Lions Gate Bridge. Southwards stand the shining sails of Canada Place and the mirrored high-rises of downtown, in sharp contrast to an eastward-stretching line of old buildings huddled along the waterfront. In 2009, the MV *Pacific Breeze* was added to the fleet, which includes the 30-year-old MV *Beaver* and the MV *Otter*, one will eventually retire from service.
After disembarking on the North Shore, turn right to Lonsdale Quay.

2 Lonsdale Quay

The ground floor of this airy glass and steel structure features a market with a colourful assortment of local and imported fruit and vegetables, meat and fish, breads and pastries, cut and dried flowers and potted plants. Inexpensive fast-food restaurants serve everything from Italian pizza to Vietnamese salad rolls. A snack, a coffee or a cold drink on the outside deck includes the stunning harbour view. The second level has a collection of gift shops and boutiques, while the third level is the entrance to the Lonsdale Quay Hotel. *West from the quay and the SeaBus Terminal lies Waterfront Park.*

3 Waterfront Park

A leisurely stroll along the meandering, wide, paved walkway takes about half an hour. Along the sea wall, signs identify prominent downtown buildings. A short wooden pier with a covered (it does rain here occasionally!) observation deck and benches juts out over the water. During the summer months, musical concerts are held here on many Sunday afternoons and, at other times, local clubs enjoy kite-flying, square-dancing, vintage car shows and native powwows. A noticeboard at the west end of the park lists events, dates and times.

Beside the walkway stands a huge series of irregular, separate steel arches spanning a shrub-covered gully, a modernistic sculpture entitled *Cathedral* by artist Douglas Senft. A little further west, an elegant, stylised sundial dominates Sailor's Point Plaza. The base of the sculpture contains tiny sketches of sunken ships. The plaza is dedicated to people who have lost their lives at sea in both peace and wartime. A plaque on the plaza celebrates Captain George Vancouver, the European who discovered and named Burrard Inlet.

Before leaving, peek through the windows of the Pacific Marine Training Institute to see the devices used by modern mariners in training.

The SeaBus runs every 15 to 30 minutes from about 6am to 1am weekdays and at half-hour intervals during the evening and some weekend time slots.
Tel: (604) 953 3333; www.translink.bc.ca

Tour: Boat ride on a bus

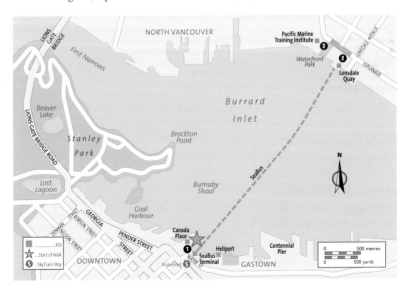

Unknown Vancouver

Although Vancouverites love their city, they sometimes take local treasures for granted, so visitors have to hunt to find them. Such local newspapers as the *Georgia Straight*, along with local radio and television stations, provide information on the area's life and leisure. Almost every weekend sees a variety of community events. There's a five-neighbourhood Lantern Festival for winter solstice, while summer brings Theatre Under the Stars – outdoor theatre in Stanley Park – and the Sandcastle Competition at Spanish Banks West Beach. Libraries often hold readings by Canadian authors, and visitors may purchase a temporary card to borrow books.

For an outdoor adventure, try picking strawberries, raspberries and blueberries in the Fraser Valley during the summer months. Salmonberries and blackberries can also be picked along many country roads and trails.

A great way to see the suburbs is to take in a garage sale. Local community newspapers list the sale venues. It is interesting to see what is sold and bought. People are very rarely in a hurry. It is, therefore, easy to strike up conversations. And you may get your Christmas or holiday shopping done early and at reduced prices.

Capilano Salmon Hatchery

The **Capilano River Regional Park** includes the Capilano River areas below the massive Cleveland Dam. Above the dam is the Capilano Lake reservoir; below lies the fish hatchery. Here you can watch salmon in various stages of growth in glass-fronted holding tanks. In the spawning season, the fish swim upstream and leap ladders into the hatchery.

4500 Capilano Park Rd, off Capilano Rd, North Vancouver. Tel: (604) 666 1790. Open: summer daily 8am–7 or 8pm; winter daily 8am–4pm. Free admission.

Cultus Lake

Golfers and watersports fans can head out to Cultus Lake, the home of Lindell Beach Holiday Resort, two hours from Vancouver. The resort offers fully equipped holiday rental homes, perfect for self-catering travellers. There's a lakeside beach, a pool and a variety of activities.
Just outside Cultus Lake on Columbia Valley Rd. Tel: (604) 624 6100,

The Capilano Lake in the picturesque Capilano River Regional Park

freephone (866) 369 6100;
www.lindellbeach.ca

Vancouver Flea Market

Bargain shopping is a favourite pastime in Vancouver, and the flea market is a mecca for junk-hunters. At this event, both junk and genuine bargains fill the display tables.
703 Terminal Ave, close to the Main St SkyTrain. Tel: (604) 685 0666; www.vancouverfleamarket.com. Open: Sat & Sun 10am–5pm, holidays 10am–4pm.

Vancouver environs

Vancouver's outlying neighbourhoods have their own distinctive characters. Richmond has authentic Chinese restaurants and Hong Kong-style shopping. West Vancouver is upmarket, with lush gardens and opulent homes. Surrey, BC's second-largest city, maintains some traditional farms and heritage parks. Many neighbourhoods can be reached by SkyTrain, facilitating an afternoon exploring parks, shopping and enjoying diversions beyond downtown.

NORTH

Across Burrard Inlet and English Bay lies Vancouver's North Shore, backed by the rugged Coast Range Mountains. Rivers, creeks and canyons meander down forested slopes, cut through clusters of houses, high-rises and businesses, and terminate along park-lined shores. Scenic coastal and mountain drives, a dozen shopping areas, a few hotels, 250 restaurants, and other businesses cater to the 200,000 North Shore residents and a much greater number of visitors (*www.cnv.org*).

The Cypress, Grouse and Seymour Mountains, visible from almost every vantage point in Vancouver, dominate the scene. So near yet so far from downtown, these city mountains provide a recreational paradise, particularly for picnics and hiking in summer and skiing in winter. When the clouds disperse, various vantage points provide spectacular views of downtown, the Gulf Islands, the American San Juan Islands and the eternal snows of distant Mount Baker.

The Capilano River and Grouse Mountain

Grouse Mountain, 1,127m (3,698ft) high (*tel: (604) 980 9311; www.grousemountain.com*), is a mere 15 minutes by car from downtown Vancouver to the big car park below the Skyride. The aerial Skyride gondola takes ten minutes to transport 100 passengers at a time up through sweeping vistas to fresh, crisp mountain air, winding trails, alpine meadows and a superb ski area.

Grouse offers a variety of top options. You can hop on a helicopter (*tel: (604) 270 1484, freephone (800) 665 4354; www.helijet.com*) and fly high across Capilano Canyon and between the peaks of The Lions. Or you can enjoy such other attractions as the Altitudes Bistro for relaxing, the elegant Observatory for high dining, and, in summer, tandem paragliding when

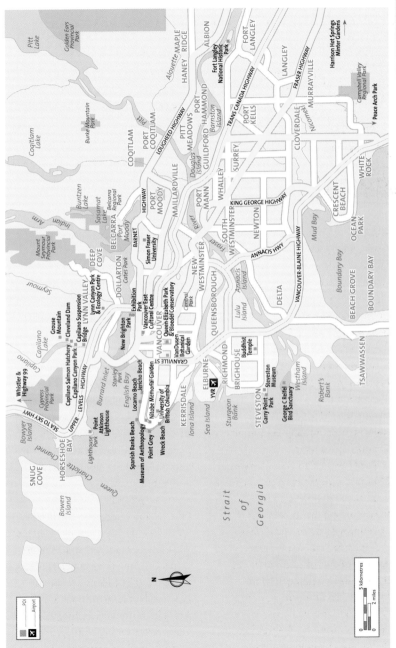

flyers jump off the mountain and glide down towards the city. At Theatre in the Sky, watch *Born to Fly*, a journey above the highest BC peaks, across Pacific Ocean white caps, and through lush green rainforest (*every hour on the hour, 10am–9pm; on the half-hour,* Animal Tracks Baby Grizzlies *is shown; admission charge*). Other excitement includes ziplines, a visit to the Refuge for Endangered Wildlife, a lumberjack show, Birds in Motion demonstration, eco walks and Eye of the Wind, a huge wind turbine. The 2.9km (1¾-mile) Grouse Grind Trail is a popular but gruelling climb 800m (2,625ft) from the mountain base.

On the way down, there are several stops worth making. The enormous Cleveland Dam, built about 40 years ago, divides the river to create Capilano Lake, which provides the city water supply. At the Capilano Salmon Hatchery (*tel: (604)*

The breathtaking aerial gondola ride up to Grouse Mountain

THE LEGEND OF THE TWO SISTERS

Renamed The Lions by the British, these twin peaks rise to 1,646m (5,400ft) at the northern end of the Cypress Provincial Park wilderness. A long time ago, as a great Capilano chief prepared to celebrate the coming of age of his twin daughters, a powerful northerly tribe declared war. But the daughters persuaded their father to invite the hostile Indians to their feast, and this potlatch festival of peace brought friendship to the tribes. The chief decided to make his daughters immortal, and lifted them to these lofty twin peaks to stand forever as symbols of peace and friendship.

666 1790), returning salmon leap ladders into the hatchery, and a display shows coho, steelhead and chinook salmon in various stages of development.

The **Capilano Suspension Bridge** (*tel: (604) 985 7474; www.capbridge.com*), the world's oldest suspension footbridge, was originally built in 1889. The wire rope and wood structure sways and flaps 70m (230ft) above the rushing waters of the river below. The bridge stretches 137m (449ft) across the steep canyon, providing access to nature trails meandering through old-growth forest. Splurge on fine dining at the Bridge House Restaurant, or grab a lunch at the Loggers' Grill or a snack at the Canyon Café. From Treetops Adventure, view the wonders of the rainforest on a series of cable suspension bridges from 30m (98ft) above the forest floor. Cliffhanger, opening in 2011, does just that from the rock face with forest views.

North Shore Mountains
Cypress Provincial Park

Northwest of Vancouver, overlooking Howe Sound to the west, Cypress Provincial Park provides spectacular views over the city to Mount Baker and southwest to Vancouver Island and the Gulf Islands. Excellent cross-country ski trails and good downhill runs attract Vancouverites every day and evening in winter – Cypress Mountain (*http://cypressmountain.com*) was the 2010 Olympic freestyle skiing and snowboard venue. In summer, the main attraction is the network of hiking trails. Some, such as the Yew Lake circuit, are suitable for novices, while the Crest Trail challenges even experts.

It takes about 20 minutes to drive to the park along the Cypress Bowl Road from Exit 8 on Upper Levels Highway (Highway 1/99). At the end of the road is a parking area, a cafeteria, a shop and the park administration building, where trail brochures are available.

Vancouver environs

The city of Vancouver against the backdrop of Mount Seymour

The evergreen forest has Douglas and amabilis fir, which thrive on this rainy coast. Alders, maples and the flowering dogwood – whose neat white blossom is the provincial flower – are deciduous. Ferns and mosses on stumps and by ageing trees, marsh marigold, skunk cabbage and salmonberries brighten the landscape. Black bears love the berries, so be sure to give them right of way. Deer feed on the open slopes along the road. The bold whisky jack lands on picnic tables, while chickadees, nuthatches, crossbills and Steller's jays forage in the forest.
Tel: (604) 926 5612.

Mount Seymour Provincial Park

This park encompasses 3,500 hectares (8,649 acres) of wilderness, including Mount Elsay and Mount Bishop, as well as Mount Seymour (1,450m/4,757ft).

Forests of old-growth fir, western red and yellow cedar, and hemlock are highlighted, with carpets of alpine flowers in open areas. Coyotes and deer range close to the road, and hares, Douglas squirrels and martens skirt the hiking trails. The backcountry is home to black bears and cougars. The guided tours and displays in the Lower Seymour Conservation Reserve (*www. metrovancouver.org/services/parks_lscr*) are an excellent way to learn about local flora and fauna, rainforests and fisheries.

The winding 13km (8-mile) Mount Seymour Road ends at parking lot 4, near the cafeteria and chairlift. The Goldie Lake/Flower Lake Trail, a Nordic ski route in winter, provides an easy and relatively flat one-hour loop, although a dozen other recommended walks are listed in the brochure available at information boards. Partway down the road, a two-hour walk along the Baden-Powell Trail leads down through thick forest and across ravines to the village of Deep Cove, on the Indian Arm, which has a sandy beach and a canoe rental shop.
Tel: (604) 986 9371.

Parks on Indian Arm

A water taxi runs across Indian Arm from Deep Cove to Belcarra Regional Park, which shelters Sasamat Lake, one of the warmest in the region. Cates Park, where the waters of Indian Arm and Burrard Inlet meet, is popular with scuba divers. A 15m (49ft) long war canoe, carved in an unusual chequerboard design, is displayed in the park. The nearby Malcolm Lowry Walk provides a peaceful ten-minute stroll through the leafy forest and back along the shell-strewn shore.
www.deepcovebc.com

Whistler

Named after the call of the hoary marmot, Whistler is a world-class winter sports centre which was the 2010 Winter Olympics venue for alpine skiers, ski jumpers, biathletes, cross-country skiers, bobsleigh, luge and skeleton teams, and Nordic events. And getting there is half the fun.

The Sea to Sky Highway

The Sea to Sky Highway, rebuilt in time for 2010 Winter Olympics traffic between Vancouver and Whistler, fringes fjord-like Howe Sound. Rugged rainforest and sheer rock faces, sculpted by glaciers during the last Ice Age, ascend to meadows blanketed in summer with Indian paintbrushes and other alpine flowers, and in winter with snow.

A good picnic place along the road is **Porteau Cove Provincial Park**, which also offers good swimming, snorkelling, scuba diving, boating and fishing. At Britannia Beach, once the largest copper producer in the British Empire and now a National Historic Site, the **BC Museum of Mining**, finishing expansion in 2011, offers underground tours in little electric trains, and an intriguing display of old mining equipment (*tel: (604) 896 2233, freephone (800) 896 4044; www.bcmm. ca; open: daily 9am–4.30pm; admission charge*).

The next stop should be **Shannon Falls Provincial Park**, where BC's third-highest waterfall thunders down a 335m (1,099ft) cliff following the trail of a slithering sea serpent, according to the local legend.

A few kilometres beyond the falls, the logging town of **Squamish** is famous as a rock-climbing centre. The Stawamus Chief, a 652m (2,139ft) high granite monolith, is the world's second largest, after the Rock of Gibraltar. Drive past reflecting lakes and through small open valleys and forest to Whistler.

Shannon Falls

Whistler: the mountain playground

Whistler Village nestles between twin Coast Range Mountain peaks, Whistler and Blackcomb. The village is a cluster of hotels, shops, condominiums, restaurants and cobbled walkways, an architectural mix of West Coast and European chalet.

A five-minute walk from the village square are the ski lifts which service the largest ski area and the two longest vertical drops on the continent: Blackcomb, 1,609m (5,279ft), and Whistler, 1,530m (5,020ft). The resort also has the most extensive high-speed ski-lift system in the world, with a total of 37 lifts and the PEAK 2 PEAK Gondola, which connects the two mountains. Cross-country trails skirt the golf course and Lost Lake. Snowboarders have five terrain parks, including a Super Pipe seen during the 2010 Winter Olympic Games. After spring sun melts winter snow, avid skiers head to the Horstman Glacier and share the lifts with mountain bikers, who ride down the gravel trails that skiers slalom in winter. At the Squamish Lil'wat Cultural Centre (*www.slcc.ca*), First Nations people demonstrate basket-making and other traditional crafts.

Whistler also offers three highly rated golf courses, hiking, horse riding, ziplining, treetop walking, canoeing, river rafting, windsurfing, fishing and helicopter flightseeing. Musicians, magicians, clowns, comedians and

HOW TO GET THERE

You can travel to Whistler, 120km (75 miles) north of Vancouver, by Helijet (*tel: (800) 665 4354; www.helijet.com*); drive yourself, which takes about two hours non-stop, or travel by train on Rocky Mountaineer's Whistler Sea to Sky Climb (*tel: (604) 606-8460; www.rockymountaineer.com*).

jugglers entertain every day in the streets from mid-June to September. Major festivals include jazz and blues in September.

Accommodation varies – though always with resort-level prices – from the luxurious Fairmont Château Whistler to the rustic Riverside RV Resort and Campground.
Freephone: (800) WHISTLER; www.whistler.com

Panorama from Whistler Mountain, looking towards Blackcomb

EAST
Lower Mainland
Fort Langley

An hour's drive east from Vancouver's chrome and glass high-rises is the historic little village of Fort Langley, the site of the original fort and fur-trading post where BC began. It was here that BC was declared a Crown Colony in 1858.

Fort Langley Village has, so far, escaped the contrived charm which often accompanies historical reconstructions. This can be attributed to the fact that most of its quaint clapboard churches, antique shops and false-fronted buildings are original.

Near the fort, the **BC Farm Museum** (*9131 King St; tel: (604) 888 2273; www.bcfma.com; open Apr–mid-Oct daily 10am–4.30pm*) houses a comprehensive collection of steam tractors, stump pullers, ploughs, reapers, harvesters, buckboards, a working sawmill and a vintage Tiger Moth plane – the first crop duster in the province.

The **Langley Centennial Museum & National Exhibition Centre** (*9135 King St; tel: (604) 888 3922; www.langleymuseum.org; open Mon–Sat 10am–4.45pm, Sun 1–4.45pm*), next door, displays Coast Salish artefacts and a selection of 19th-century pioneer crafts and furnishings.

Fort Langley National Historic Site

First built in 1827, then relocated and rebuilt twice in 1839 and 1840, Fort Langley was once the Hudson's Bay Company's most important provisioning post in the Pacific Northwest, and has been reconstructed to re-create the past. Within the palisaded high wooden walls, the Big House, the bastion, a cooperage and carpentry shop, and a blacksmith's forge have been rebuilt. The storehouse, the only original structure on-site, is stacked with furs, clothing, trapping equipment, trading goods and other supplies used by fur traders, gold miners, Indians and other 19th-century residents.

Interpreters in period costumes demonstrate pioneer life at the fort. Some are blacksmiths fashioning tools; some are coopers building barrels, which were once used to ship salmon and other foodstuffs from the fort; and some bake salmon and bannock in open outdoor ovens.

(*Cont. on p88*)

THE HUDSON'S BAY COMPANY

This company of English adventurers formed in 1670, during the reign of King Charles II, to trade throughout the lands that had rivers which drained into Hudson's Bay.

The commercial empire that grew out of it began with a few shiploads of British goods being traded for furs, and at one time it was the largest landowner in the world. After Canada became a nation, in 1869 the Hudson's Bay Company gave up its trade monopoly, but retained its forts and trading posts. Eventually, a chain of Hudson's Bay department stores was built in western Canada and still exists today under the store name, the Bay.

Animal kingdom

Vancouver is a little like Sleeping Beauty – blessed by the good fairies at birth with great natural beauty everywhere. The city rests at the foot of a range of mountains and looks out to the ocean with deep inlets cutting into the land. Parks and gardens are scattered everywhere through the city, and pristine rainforest and wilderness lie just behind the last row of houses on the North Shore. Vancouverites proudly coexist harmoniously (most of the time) with critters from the forest.

In North Vancouver, signs in the parks warn of wandering bears, and local dogs stroll along wearing 'bear bells'. It's not unusual for a local matron to step outside on to the doorstep for her morning paper and see a bear walking up the driveway. Most of the time these natural

Vancouver's many pockets of wilderness are a delight for animal lovers

An elk in the Rockies

encounters are uneventful, but once a cougar wandered into Victoria and was seen prowling around the car park of the city's most famous hotel.

Raccoons seem to hang out wherever there's a small stand of natural park, and in the city they can be a real nuisance on 'garbage day' along with legions of chipmunks, skunks and squirrels. Vancouver's Stanley Park, a thickly wooded tract of cedar, hemlock and fir, has its own battalion of raccoons that will shamelessly beg for chips or popcorn. Park officials discourage visitors from feeding these beggars since they may bite. Even more dangerous are the minefields of poop left by the park's beautiful but messy Canada geese. Coyotes are the most recent arrival for concern in many Vancouver parks.

In the Fraser Valley to the east of the city and beyond, you can see fields of ordinary farm animals. More exotic species such as llamas and alpacas are also being raised as pets, for their wool or as guide animals. On a train ride further into the province, there's a good chance of spotting a herd of bighorn sheep grazing by the tracks.

On the Gulf Islands and on Vancouver Island deer can be so numerous that they are considered to be pests.

A costumed interpreter at Fort Langley National Historic Site

Other interpreters narrate fort history and organise games to help children enjoy learning local history. Coast Salish native people from neighbouring MacMillan Island often work at the fort constructing canoes, carving paddles and making jewellery.

The Big House replicates the original building which was pulled down in 1886. The refurbished parlour suggests the relative luxury the chief trader and his family enjoyed, and an intriguing diary displayed in the big hall describes early life at the fort.

Brigade Days, held in early August, re-enact the fur brigades arriving to trade at Fort Langley after weeks of canoeing south through networks of rivers. Douglas Day, in mid-November, is another colourful ceremony, which commemorates the inauguration of BC.

The Friends of the Fort gift shop stocks a variety of souvenirs, including reproductions of old trading goods. *23433 Mavis St. Tel: (604) 513 4777. www.pc.gc.ca. Open: Jul–Aug daily 9am–8pm; Sept–Jun daily 10am–5pm. Admission charge.*

MV *Native* riverboat trip

A pleasant way to visit Fort Langley is aboard MV *Native*, a working replica of a late 19th-century paddle wheeler. This 100-passenger vessel follows the Fraser River upstream from New Westminster to Fort Langley.

The four-hour journey traces the route taken by fortune hunters, fur traders, miners, merchants, millionaires and stagecoach robbers during the 19th century. First Nations people canoed the route while fishing, hunting and trapping. The excursion is narrated, with extracts by early explorers. The company runs both lunch and dinner cruises.

900 Quayside, New Westminster.
Tel: (604) 525 4465,
freephone (877) 825 1302;
www.vancouverpaddlewheeler.com

Harrison Hot Springs

These hot springs were discovered rather dramatically during the 1850s when a clumsy prospector was tipped out of his canoe into Harrison Lake. He was dumbfounded to find the water not frigid, but warm. Word spread and, for later prospectors on the Gold Rush Trail, Harrison Hot Springs became a popular stopover site.

Although Harrison Hot Springs Hotel is today in the luxury category, anyone can enjoy such specialities as lobster mousse or poached salmon in the restaurant and look out at the lake. There is also plenty of less expensive hotel, motel and campground accommodation. Other restaurants line the lake shore.

Shoppers and browsers can enjoy a range of shops offering everything from video rentals and camping supplies to Canadiana.

Soothing spring waters

Two springs percolate from the base of nearby mountains. A sulphur spring, about two-thirds sodium sulphate and sodium chloride, flows out at 62°C (144°F). A potash spring, with potassium chloride and sodium sulphate making up more than half its mineral content, enters the lake at 40°C (104°F). Both spring waters also contain lime and magnesium sulphates, sulphurated hydrogen and bicarbonates of lime and iron. To see the springs bubbling up from their source, walk westwards along the dyke beside the lake and past the hotel.

A pipe system carries the mineral waters to the hotel and public pools, for which there is an admission charge. The water is stored in huge tanks and cooled to 38°C (100°F), the perfect temperature for a soothing soak. Massages are available.

Outdoor activities and sport

The town of Harrison Hot Springs offers a great variety of outdoor activities. Boaters explore the lake, which stretches 60km (37 miles) north – watch for strong thermal winds which may rise rapidly shortly after noon on a summer day. The morning calm is great for waterskiing, and the afternoon winds are great for windsurfing. Other outdoor options include fishing, golf, tennis, cycling, croquet, horseshoes and shuffleboard.

Numerous walking and hiking trails provide easy access to the forests and mountains. The easiest one, about 2km (1¼ miles) long, follows the lake from the Harrison Hot Springs Hotel to the boat launch and around the lagoon, while the Campbell Lake Trail, which requires more than four hours, rises a challenging 600m (1,969ft) to a beautiful mountain lake.

A sand sculpture competition in early September attracts many visitors to Harrison Hot Springs every year; the record for the world's tallest sandcastle was set here in 1990.

There is a parade of gaily lit boats on the lake during the evening of 1 July, Canada Day. The week-long Festival of the Arts (*www.harrisonfestival.com*), later in July, features a spectrum of artistic expression in music, dance, theatre and visual art. A special day set aside for

children includes storytellers, face-painting, workshops and other activities, and a Literary Café writer's evening offers readings with Canadian authors. *Tel: (604) 796 5581; www.tourismharrison.com, www.harrisonfestival.com*

Minter Gardens
Tucked away a few metres west off Yale Road, just after the turn-off north from Highway 1 to Harrison Hot Springs, are the Minter Gardens. Pathways wind through 11 hectares (27 acres) of sights, sounds, fragrances, textures and tastes. In springtime, tulips, daffodils, hyacinths, primulas, rhododendrons and azaleas blaze with colour. Summer brings a prize display of annuals, and autumn presents a

Minter Gardens are a riot of flowers in the summer

shower of falling leaves in green, gold and red, against the backdrop 2,134m (7,001ft) Mount Cheam. The Rose Garden blooms most of the year, and there are topiaries, a rare collection of Penjing rock bonsai, and a fragrance trail for blind visitors.
Tel: (604) 794 7191,
freephone (888) 646 8377;
www.mintergardens.com. Open: late
Mar–mid-Oct daily, call for times.
Admission charge.

Peace Arch Park

Canada, the second-largest country in area on earth (after Russia), and the USA have the longest undefended international border in the world, stretching 6,500km (4,040 miles) from the Atlantic Ocean to the Pacific. Shared by both countries, the Peace Arch Park at the southern end of Highway 99 in BC may be one of the most beautiful border crossings anywhere.

A monument to peace

The idea of a peace arch was conceived by the late Samuel Hill of Seattle to commemorate a permanent peace between Canada and the USA. While President of the Pacific Highway Association, Hill, a road builder and Quaker, proposed that an arch be constructed at the centenary of the signing of the Treaty of Ghent in 1814, which marked the end of the War of 1812 between Great Britain and the USA, resolving the ongoing conflict between the two powers at that time.

The Peace Arch, the first such structure in the world, became a reality in 1921 and also marked the 300th anniversary of the sailing of the Pilgrim Fathers to America.

Built of concrete reinforced with steel, in Greek Doric style, the arch was designed to vibrate but not crack in case of an earthquake. The gleaming white open portal, which stands about 30m (98ft) high, flies the Canadian and American flags side by side. Across the top on the American side is the inscription 'Children of a Common Mother'. The Canadian side reads 'Brethren Dwelling Together in Unity'.

Two iron gates span the opening that leads from one country to the other. Children and adults from both countries like to stand here, with one foot planted on Canadian soil, the other in the USA. In a celebration held in early June every year, children from both countries meet and file through the portal to exchange flags. Over the west gate is written '1814 – Open for One Hundred Years – 1914' and over the east 'May These Gates Never Be Closed'.

Originally incorporated into a hollow arch cornerstone was a beam from the SS *Beaver*, which in 1836 became the first steamship to enter the Pacific Ocean, along with a piece of wooden hull from the *Mayflower*, the ship that carried the pilgrims to America in 1621.

A garden of harmony

During the 1920s, some peace-lovers banded together to raise funds to

The Peace Arch, which symbolically bridges the national boundary between Canada and the USA

purchase land surrounding the Peace Arch for a park. BC schoolchildren responded, some with only a penny, others with as much as 10 cents. More than $2,000 was raised, a considerable sum in those days. The money was used to purchase a portion of the property. Other funds were eventually found and 9 hectares (22 acres) were set aside as the Peace Arch Park. The 7 hectares (17 acres) that make up the Washington State Peace Arch Park were eventually acquired in a similar fashion.

Today, the Peace Arch serves as a symbol to remind all passing by that neighbours can live together in peace. The portal is the centrepiece of the surrounding broad green lawns, flower gardens, rockeries, playgrounds, picnic areas, shelters and kitchens that have been built on both sides over the years. The Canadian side features a wooden gazebo, a lily pond and a rectangle of red and white flowers representing the Canadian flag. To the west, a cliff overlooks the old Burlington Northern Railway line and the waters of Semiahmoo Bay, which wash the shores of both countries.
www.env.gov.bc.ca/bcparks/explore/ parks

SOUTH
Steveston

A half-hour drive (32km/20 miles) south from downtown Vancouver is Steveston (within Richmond city limits) at the mouth of the mighty

Fraser. The river boasts the biggest salmon run in North America, and Steveston has the largest fleet of commercial fishing vessels on Canada's West Coast. **Moncton Street** has seafood restaurants, marine supply stores, antique shops, galleries and shopping.

Garry Point Park

A five-minute walk west lies sandy, windswept Garry Point Park, with views of the Fraser River and Gulf Islands. A tiny oriental garden, beside the broad walking path, commemorates the arrival of the first Japanese immigrants more than a century ago.

Gulf of Georgia Cannery National Historic Site

Giving an insight into the fishing industry, the intact 1894–1964 cannery complex shows how this major West Coast fishery processed and canned catches of salmon, herring and halibut. *12138 4th Ave (Richmond). Tel: (604) 664 9009; www.pc.gc.ca. Open: Feb–Oct daily 10am–5pm.*

Steveston Museum

Here a collection of fishing, farming and blacksmithing tools used by early Japanese settlers is on display. Some rooms in the 1906 structure have been restored, and contain period furniture. *3811 Moncton St. Tel: (604) 718 8439. Open: Mon–Sat 9.30am–1pm & 1.30–5pm.*

Flowers in season

When most people think of BC they envisage a land blanketed in greenery. The Lower Mainland region does tend to remain eternally leafy, thanks to the temperate climate and abundant rains.

It is usually March when the first crocuses, daffodils, tulips and hyacinths burst forth. Bold umbrellas of pink unfold on Japanese cherry trees along city streets; magnolias and camellias bloom in delicate whites and pinks, and the japonica bushes open bright clusters of flowers resembling apple blossoms. Forsythia shrubs produce golden streamers and wisterias wind long tassels of purple along building walls. Yellow skunk cabbages, which smell like they sound, brighten dank forest areas in Stanley Park.

In June, azaleas and rhododendrons, dressed in brilliant hues of pink, salmon, coral and crimson, announce the advent of summer. Roses bloom in town and country gardens, and wild lupines brighten the roadsides. Dahlias, delphiniums, phlox, asters and poppies share the summer sun with sweet peas, gladioli, freesias, zinnias, marigolds and nasturtiums, while fuchsias and busy Lizzies thrive in the shade. Moss-packed hanging baskets sport trailing lobelias and verbenas, mingled with petunias and pelargoniums.

The late summer display includes snapdragons, primroses, wallflowers and Canterbury bells. As the golden autumn leaves fall from the trees, irises, cat's tails (or reed mace) and

Summer months bring a riot of nicotiana

From spring to late summer, BC's gardens and parks are always in full bloom

marsh marigolds begin to flower near ponds and lakes.

Even the grey winter is brightened by flowering plants. Clumps of white and pink heather border lawns, while window boxes appear colourful with winter pansies and curly kale. Some roses, along with the pretty blossoms of the winter-flowering plum and the yellow trumpets of winter jasmine, bloom right through a short snowfall. Holly outside and poinsettias inside follow the Christmas tradition of red and green. Red-osier dogwoods, the bright yellow twigs of Siberian dogwood and clusters of bright pink berries on the spindleberry bush also liven the winter landscape.

en Island lies northwest of Vancouver. A 20-minute
ride on the Queen of Capilano *from Horseshoe Bay*
nug Cove, it makes a wonderful day trip from
ouver. This lush, green, bowl-shaped isle, capped by
n (2,493ft) Mount Gardner, has long been a holiday
away or day trip for Vancouverites.

Allow a day for the trip.

From Vancouver, the journey to Horseshoe Bay takes half an hour by car; head northwest along Georgia St, across the Lions Gate Bridge and follow the ferry signs west along the Upper Levels Highway. There is usually ample parking in Horseshoe Bay, except on holiday weekends. A car is not necessary on the island; board the ferry (BC Ferries; www.bcferries.com) as a foot passenger.

To reach Horseshoe Bay from downtown Vancouver by bus, allow an hour. Take the Blue Bus (tel: (604) 985 7777) on Georgia St, which runs every half-hour to Horseshoe Bay. Bus No 250 follows scenic Marine Dr through West Vancouver and Bus No 257 follows the highway. For more information, tel: (250) 947 9024; www.bowenchamber.com

As the ferry rounds the point from Horseshoe Bay into Queen Charlotte Sound, the Lions and the Howe Sound Crest Mountains appear dramatically outlined against the sky. South across

the water lies little Passage Island, Point Atkinson Lighthouse and, across English Bay, Point Grey.

From the ferry dock in Snug Cove, it is a three-minute walk along Government Road to the commercial centre of the island.

This main square has a couple of pubs, restaurants with flower-decked patios, craft shops and bakeries; break here for a coffee and a snack before embarking on the walk. The square also boasts the restored Union Steamship Company Store, which is now the local library. It's just a short walk from the store to the Visitor Information Centre at 432 Cardena Road.

Detour right before the store where a short, tree-lined road leads to a freshwater lagoon and the calm waters of Deep Bay. Opposite Cardena Dr, a green sign indicates a leafy trail that marks the entrance to Crippen Regional Park and the Killarney Lake Trail.

It is a 6km (3¾-mile) round trip. The trail is wide and fairly flat, except for a few steep sections. For a leisurely stroll, allow about two hours.

A few minutes along the trail, the sound of plunging Terminal Creek announces two fish ladders zigzagging up the rocky hillside beside the creek. During October and November, salmon that went to sea after being raised in a nearby hatchery return after two or three years to leap the ladders upstream and spawn in the waters they came from.

The trail, flanked by trees, emerges on to Miller Road shortly after the fish ladders. About 100m (328ft) to the right, the trail continues on the other side. Red cedars, hemlocks and maples tower over a tangled undergrowth where huge stumps still remain as reminders of earlier logging activity.

The trail crosses Magee Road to the Killarney Lake Loop Trail, where bikes and horses are not allowed because the terrain needs protection from overuse. The main trail heads north around the lake to a gravel beach with picnic tables, toilets and a small swimming area. The trail climbs slightly to join a broad boardwalk over a marsh where Labrador tea, bog laurel, sweet gale bushes and the carnivorous sundew plant thrive. In early summer brilliant yellow (and appropriately named) skunk cabbage glows in the underbrush. Blue herons hunch in the shallow water. The trail meanders on, with frequent views of the lake and the forested foothills around Mount Gardner.

Follow the signs to Snug Cove to catch the ferry back to the mainland.

Walk: Bowen Island

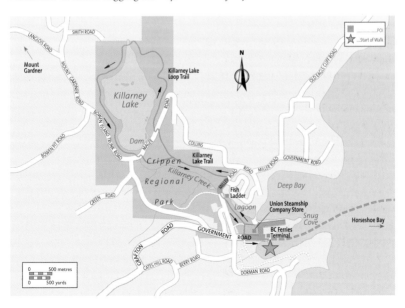

WEST

Mention West Vancouver and most Canadians conjure up images of sprawling, million-dollar waterfront mansions backed by park-like gardens, and driveways filled with Mercedes and Jaguars. It is true that the municipality's 42,000 residents may boast the highest per capita income in Canada. The best-known luxurious residential area is called The British Properties. But many small clapboard cottages, built as summer homes long before the Guinness family built the Lions Gate Bridge in 1938, still survive here untouched by developers, and are valued at prices far lower than the current value of the land they occupy.

West Vancouver is not the Wild West. More than 20 per cent of West Vaners are pensioned senior citizens. There is little crime and no industry. The suburb snakes for 20km (12 miles) along the north shore of English Bay from the Lions Gate Bridge to Horseshoe Bay, and climbs about 5km (3 miles) up the slope towards Cypress Mountain. West Vancouver has over 100 parks and over 100km (62 miles) of paths and trails connecting the community. Once people have lived here, they say they would not want to live anywhere else in Canada, even though commuters encounter frequent waits in summer to cross the bridge to the big city.

For browsing or buying, West Vancouver has the Park Royal Shopping Centre (*www.shopparkroyal.com*) and a good range of little stores in Ambleside Village and in the one block between 24th and 25th Streets called Dundarave Village (*www.dundaravevillage.ca*). Visitors can also enjoy fishing, golfing, tennis at free public courts, lawn bowling, swimming and exercise at several fitness circuits.

Ferry Building

Built in 1913, this heritage building, which is now a waterfront gallery, was once a meeting place for residents arriving from and leaving for downtown Vancouver. The adjacent waterfront park, known as Ambleside Landing, offers a view of Prospect Point in Stanley Park, and features a fountain sculpture and a fishing pier with a cleaning table.

1414 Argyle Ave. Tel: (604) 925 7290; http://ferrybuildinggallery.com. Open: Tue–Sun 11am–5pm.

Gertrude Lawson House

Home to the **West Vancouver Museum** and Archives, this ballast-stone house was built in 1940 by Gertrude Lawson, daughter of the Father of West Vancouver, businessman John Lawson. It is now a museum relating the history of the area. The unusual stone façade of the house echoes the architectural character of the grand homes of Scotland, which Ms Lawson greatly admired. The stones are themselves believed to have come from New Zealand as ballast on timber trading ships.

680 17th St. Tel: (604) 925 7295; http://westvancouvermuseum.ca. Open: Tue–Sat 11am–5pm. Admission by donation.

Parks and walkways

In West Vancouver, gardens, parks and walkways are everywhere. Ambleside Park is a great place to see residents walking their dogs. The spectacular 1.7km (1-mile) paved sea walk has a fenced-off trail for dogs. The best beach is the little one east of Dundarave Pier, between 14th and Bellevue, where concession stands sell summer snacks for beachcombers. This is also a popular place for summer crabbing and fishing. Westwards, a pebbled shore strewn with driftwood, is a great place for beachcombing. Caulfield Park, which has a forested path along the waterfront, is famous for its flush toilets!

Lighthouse Park, a treasure hidden away further west along Marine Drive, has a labyrinth of trails through a forest of giant Douglas firs, pines, hemlocks and arbutus trees, recognisable by their smooth, peeling rust-red bark. The Point Atkinson Lighthouse, built in 1912, is one of the few working lighthouses left in the province. The promontory just west of the lighthouse offers views of freighters anchored in English Bay, Point Grey and the mountains of Vancouver Island.

Vancouver environs

Lions Gate Bridge spans Burrard Inlet, linking downtown Vancouver with the North Shore

Vancouver's islands

Almost 200 islands lie between the Lower Mainland and Vancouver Island (see map p104). Some offer superb natural scenery, outdoor activities, accommodation and food. Although locals love the quiet winters on the islands, they are much livelier in summer when visitors come from all over the world for the spectacular water views, the balmy climate, the abundant sunshine and the calm lifestyle.

For more information visit www.vancouverisland.travel

GULF ISLANDS

The six major inhabited Gulf Islands are **Galiano**, **Mayne**, **North** and **South Pender**, **Salt Spring** and **Saturna**. Salt Spring is the most developed and the most densely populated. Mayne is preferred by many visitors.

Popular Gulf Island activities include swimming, scuba diving, fishing, canoeing, kayaking, clam digging, beachcombing, hiking and cycling, although the islands are popular precisely because there is relatively little organised activity.

Most of the Gulf Islands are accessible year-round via BC Ferries (*tel: (888) 223 3779 or (250) 386 3431; www.bcferries.com*) and Harbour Air (*freephone (800) 665 0212; www.harbour-air.com*). Ferries to the islands leave from Tsawwassen, on the mainland 29km (18 miles) south of Vancouver. Boaters prefer to visit in their own craft, finding shelter and moorage at numerous bays throughout the islands. The Gulf Islands National Park Reserve (*www.pc.gc.ca*) protects sections of many islands.

Galiano Island

Coon Bay, Bluffs Park, Mount Sutil and Mount Galiano have fine views. Montague Harbour Marine Provincial Park offers birdwatching and picnicking (*for more information see www.galianoisland.com*).

Mayne Island

Mayne Island has only 1,100 year-round residents, mostly artists and artisans, a few businesspeople, and others who have retired to enjoy a leisurely island lifestyle.

Like the other Gulf Islands, Mayne is mainly bays and beaches, and gentle wooded hills of arbutus, Douglas fir, alder, cedar and brilliant bursts of broom, although early settlers did clear some land for farming.

While its wilderness is wonderful, Mayne Island offers interesting history as well. First Nations tribes inhabited

Helen Point 5,000 years ago. Evidence remains in the middens and white beaches formed from eroded clam, abalone and oyster shells. In the late 1850s, rowdy miners stopped here en route from Victoria to the goldfields of Barkerville; some returned to enjoy the relatively mild winters. At the turn of the last century, British gentry liked to spend their summers on Mayne.

The lighthouse at Georgina Point, built in 1885, still guides vessels into the eastern entrance to Active Pass. The lighthouse, known as the Active Pass Lighthouse, is not open, but the grounds are open for visitors.

The best-loved country church on Mayne Island is St Mary Magdalene's, built in 1898 on a hill overlooking Active Pass. The 180kg (397lb)

For more information on the Gulf Islands, contact Tourism Vancouver Island, *501-65 Front St, Nanaimo. Tel: (250) 754 3500; www.vancouverisland.travel. Also see www.gulfislandstourism.com*

sandstone font was carried by rowing boat from Saturna Island in 1900.

The Mayne Island (Miners Bay) Gaol is open in summer (free admission). Built in 1896, it is now a museum housing 19th-century memorabilia, including remnants from the sailing barque *Zephyr*, which sank in 1872, when it hit the Georgina shoals.

Mayne Island Kayaking (*tel: (250) 539 0439; www.kayakmayneisland.com*) rents kayaks and leads interpretive kayak tours. Most Mayne roads are hilly, but asphalted. Rent a bike for a

Vancouver's islands

Vancouver's islands have many sheltered bays for fishing boats and pleasure craft

day of pleasant touring to see most of the island. Get natural eats at Happy Tides (*Mayne Mall; tel: (250) 539 2122*) or find something locally grown at the seasonal farmer's market.
Check out *www.mayneislandchamber.ca*

Pender Islands

Famous for beaches and coves as well as for their wildlife. On North Pender, the Driftwood Centre and craft shops at Port Washington are another attraction. The New Year's Eve Lantern Festival and Fall Fair in September at the community centre, with its bear totem poles, are major events.
www.penderisland.info,
www.penderislandchamber.com

Salt Spring Island

Look out for art and craft galleries, village shops and the Saturday-morning market at Ganges. Views at Mount Maxwell and Ruckle Provincial Parks are superb.
Events: Round the Island Race (May); Sea Capers (Jun); Art/Craft Exhibition (Jun–Sept); Fall Fair (Sept).
www.saltspringisland.org;
www.saltspringtourism.com

Saturna Island

East Point Lighthouse, Saturna pub and store, and Winter Cove Marine Park are all worth a visit. Wildlife, including ravens and wild goats, can be seen.
Events: Lamb Barbecue (Jul).
www.saturnatourism.com

Haida craftsman at work

HAIDA GWAII (QUEEN CHARLOTTE ISLANDS)

Haida Gwaii, the First Nations Haida name for what (until 2009) had been known as the Queen Charlotte Islands, include two main islands, Graham and Moresby, and 150 smaller ones. They lie northwest of Vancouver Island and about 120km (72 miles) west of Prince Rupert (*see map on p21*). Often hidden by a grey blanket of cloud and fog, Haida Gwaii is surrounded by treacherous seas and rocks. The Cape St James weather station, hugging the southern tip of the southernmost island, is the windiest in Canada. But it is also the warmest, thanks to the Kuroshio Current, which crosses the Pacific Ocean from Japan.

In 1993, the Gwaii Haanas National Park Reserve and Haida Heritage Site (*reservations: tel: (877) 559 8818;*

www.pc.gc.ca) was established to preserve Haida heritage sites and sacred areas. Access to areas and sites is quite restricted and visitors to heritage areas must, through a tour operator or directly, reserve, pay the park entry fee and attend an orientation session.

Much of empty **Moresby Island** is parkland, a result of efforts by Haida and other environmentalists. Although the Haida are fishermen by tradition, the 2,000 who live here today are celebrated for beautifully carved wooden masks, canoes, totem poles, and smaller items shaped in argillite (black slate). About 8,000 Haida once lived here, and they were famed as fierce warriors. They were decimated by diseases, probably beginning in 1774, when the first European, Juan José Pérez, sailed round the northern coast.

Grey, weathered totem poles still stand at several abandoned villages throughout these rugged isles. Tours by boat, sailboat and kayak may go to SGaang Gwaii (Ninstints) on Anthony Island, site of the largest cluster of original standing totem poles in the world, Skedans, or to T'annu, where moss has overtaken house pits.

Although about 5,000 people in all now live in Haida Gwaii, there are no shopping malls. The isolation and the mists have, over the years, attracted many interesting characters, some who came to the islands because they were different, and others who became different because they came to the islands.

The moss-draped forests of the Galapagos North, as Haida Gwaii is sometimes called, provide a dreamy silence for the shy black-tailed deer, Roosevelt elk and black bear that live in them. On the eastern shores, where the murmuring sea washes broad crescents of pebbles and sand, loons call soulfully over the waters and bald eagles squeal overhead from shadowing stands of ancient cedar and Sitka spruce. Whales, sea lions, porpoises and puffins live offshore. Anglers usually go home with catches of rock and ling cod, salmon, halibut, trout and red snapper. The economy has changed in recent years: fishing remains a strong industry, but logging is fast disappearing.

For more information see
www.haidagwaiitourism.ca

Delkatla Wildlife Sanctuary

Birdwatchers flock to see more than 100 native and migrating bird species

HOW TO GET THERE

Air Canada jets twice daily in summer from Vancouver to Sandspit on northeast Moresby Island. Pacific Coastal Airlines flies from Vancouver to Masset. You can also fly North Pacific Seaplanes from Prince Rupert Masset Marina, or the villages of Queen Charlotte or Sandspit. Getting around the islands is difficult and car rental expensive. BC Ferries (*www.bcferries.com*) makes the six-hour run from Prince Rupert to Skidegate. A 25-minute ferry runs every hour or two between Moresby Island and Graham Island, where most of the relatively small selection of motels and hotels are located.

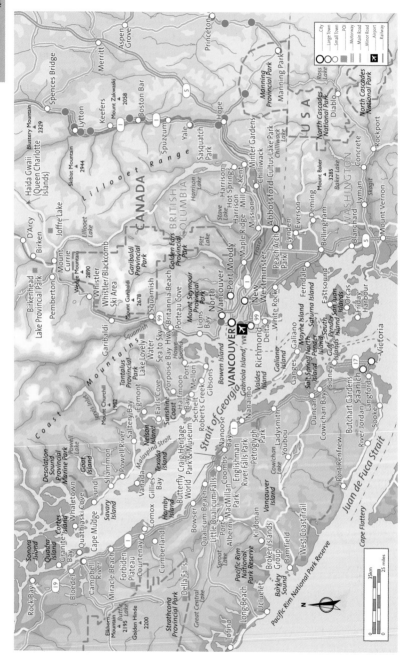

that have been spotted here, including auklets, petrels, puffins and sandhill cranes.

On a salt marsh west of Masset and Naikoon Park, Graham Island. www.massetbc.com. Open: summer.

Haida Heritage Centre

The Haida Heritage Centre at Kaay Llnagaay on Graham Island includes a series of traditional Haida cedar longhouses. The modern replicas serve as a home for Haida culture and a place to learn and share Haida life. This complex includes monumental totem poles, modern work, historical Haida art and photo archives. Events include Skidegate Days in July, and seafood dinners followed by traditional Haida dances.

Tel: (250) 559 7885; www.haidaheritagecentre.com. Open: year-round, call for dates and times. Admission charge.

Naikoon Provincial Park

Naikoon (meaning 'rose point' in Haida) Provincial Park offers 100km (62 miles) of beaches. It contains many hiking trails, including one to Tow Hill, which overlooks an agate beach and an unusual lava formation. Sitka deer and the rare Peale's peregrine falcon can be spotted here.

On the east coast between Tlell and Masset, Graham Island. Tel: (250) 626 5115. Open: daily. Parking fee.

QUADRA ISLAND

Quadra Island lies off Vancouver Island's northeast coast, just a ten-minute ferry ride across Discovery Passage from the salmon-fishing centre of Campbell River.

In addition to First Nations culture and regional cuisine, the island offers many options for outdoor recreation, including kayaking, canoeing, scuba diving, whale-watching and fishing.

Landlubbers can enjoy beachcombing at Rebecca Spit, hiking the trails or climbing up Chinese Mountain for the spectacular view, and mountain biking.

For history buffs, there are interesting ruins to explore at the Lucky Jim Mine, and ancient Indian petroglyphs or stone drawings at Francisco Point, We-wai-kai Beach and Cape Mudge.

Nuyumbalees Cultural Centre

The Potlatch Collection at the Nuyumbalees Cultural Centre at Cape Mudge Village features sacred Kwa'Kwa'Ka' Wa'Kw ceremonial objects such as masks, headdresses, coppers and other regalia used in winter ceremonies. There's a vintage photograph collection, gift shop and, on a nearby beach, over 50 ancient petroglyphs.

37 Weway Rd, Cape Mudge. Tel: (250) 285 3733. www.nuyumbalees.com. Open: May–Sept daily 9am–5pm; Oct–Apr Mon–Sat 9am–5pm. Admission charge.

HOW TO GET THERE

There are regular scheduled flights from Vancouver Airport to Campbell River, and a daily floatplane service from Coal Harbour to Campbell River.

VANCOUVER ISLAND

Islands conjure up all kinds of images, and Vancouver Island is no exception. Stretching 450km (280 miles) along Canada's Pacific Coast, this huge island brings to mind images of mossy, dense and dark rainforests of fir, cedar and hemlock; barren, wind- and surf-swept Pacific beaches; Edwardian lampposts draped with baskets of trailing flowers; and elegant Victorian afternoon teas.

Victoria

Although BC is no longer predominantly British, Victoria, the provincial capital, which began as a Hudson's Bay trading post in 1843, still retains some elements of British life – traditional afternoon tea, and a sense of propriety and order. Victorians, like many island people, tend to be relaxed and understanding. Perhaps this is because the sun shines more than in Vancouver, a mere 100km (62 miles) north.

With its historic buildings, colourful old Chinatown, museums and lovely parks and gardens, Victoria offers visitors much to see and do. But for a different way to see the city, Victoria Carriage Tours (*tel: (250) 383 2207, freephone (877) 663 2207; www. victoriacarriage.com*) has a vintage carriage drawn by a single white horse.

Alternatively, take a harbour cruise, go fishing, or have afternoon tea at the Fairmont Empress (*tel: (250) 384 8111; www.fairmont.com/empress*), or at one of several other tea rooms around Victoria.

Butchart Gardens

Possibly the most spectacular floral display on the continent today, these gardens began as an abandoned limestone quarry in 1904. Meandering paved pathways lead through 22 hectares (55 acres) of exquisite arrangements of more than 5,000 varieties of trees, shrubs and flowers. There is a sunken garden, rose garden, Japanese garden, Italian garden, star pond, concert lawn, fireworks basin, show greenhouse, seed store, two restaurants and a coffee bar. An ecotour boat plies local waters for a different perspective on the gardens,

and children have an animal menagerie carousel.

In summer, entertainment includes puppet shows, night illuminations and fireworks, while in winter, ribbons of lights brighten the grey days. Wheelchairs, baby pushcarts and umbrellas are available.

800 Benvenuto Ave, about 21km (13 miles) north of Victoria via Highway 17 and Keating Cross Rd. Freephone: (866) 652 4422; www.butchartgardens.com. Open: daily 9am. Closing times vary – call or visit website.

The Butchart Gardens, north of Victoria, are a showcase of floral displays

Helmcken House

The oldest house in BC open to the public was built in 1852. It provides a glimpse into the life of a pioneer physician 150 years ago. The house is part of the Royal BC Museum.

251 Superior St. Contact the Royal BC Museum, tel: (250) 356 7226, freephone (888) 447 7977; www.royalbcmuseum.bc.ca for visit schedule.

Parliament Buildings

Hourly tours show off this stately grey stone structure and its intricate stained-glass windows, Italian marble panels, mosaic tile floors and painted murals illustrating the province's farming, fishing, mining and logging past.

On the Inner Harbour. See www.leg.bc.ca/_media/flash/Place.pdf. Open: May–Sept daily 9am–5pm; Oct–Apr Mon–Fri 9am–5pm.

Royal BC Museum

The Royal BC Museum rates for many as the finest museum in Canada, with displays of BC history which include a woolly mammoth, cobblestone streets bordered by Victorian storefronts, a working gold-rush waterwheel, a replica of Captain George Vancouver's ship *Discovery* and a superb display and interpretation of First Nations' masks and totem poles.

675 Belleville St. Tel: (250) 356 7226; www.royalbcmuseum.bc.ca. Open: daily 10am–5pm. Admission charge.

Thunderbird Park

This downtown park has an outdoor display of replicas of old totem poles and original contemporary poles, a clan house and carvings by coastal First Nations artists.

Beside Helmcken House.

For information on other attractions and activities, visit the Tourism Victoria Visitor Centre, at *812 Wharf St. Tel: (250) 953 2033; www.tourismvictoria.com*

BC's birdlife

With a huge variety of native species, from seabirds to snow geese, BC holds a great attraction for birdwatchers

Both ornithologists and amateur naturalists love BC birdwatching, one of the fastest-growing recreational activities in the province. BC is home to more than 460 species of birds, representing more than 80 per cent of all the species found in Canada. Being less elusive than other wildlife in BC, birds are relatively easy to spot, to identify and to watch. Their distinctive cries and tuneful songs are another attraction.

The easily accessible Lower Mainland region is home to numerous species of birds, while others winter here to escape the northern Arctic winds and snows, and still others stop to feed and rest during annual migrations.

In Vancouver, some elderly West End residents make a weekly ritual of greeting and feeding the ducks and swans around Lost Lagoon, on the fringe of Stanley Park. Park traffic sometimes stops to allow a gaggle of Canada geese to cross the road. At the rocky cliffs near Siwash Rock, cormorants, gulls and guillemots make their nests, and within the forest bald eagles can be seen perched on tall trees.

Kingfishers and great blue herons are often seen hunting at Coal Harbour, Vancouver Island, along with loons, whose lonesome yodel seems to echo the solitude of the Canadian wilderness.

Iona Island, in Richmond, is a good place to observe grebes, ducks, hawks, owls and passerines, while Pitt Meadows, in the Fraser Valley, is home to green herons, ducks, sandhill cranes, hawks and owls. But the best place for birdwatching is probably the Reifel Bird Sanctuary (*www.reifelbirdsanctuary.com*), located on the swampy, salty delta of the Fraser River. This area is home to Canada's largest concentration of waterfowl, including about 40,000 snow geese. The birds are best seen here from September to May.

Rare Bird Alert (*tel: (604) 737 3074*) provides details of rare birds sighted in the Greater Vancouver area. Rare bird sightings are also posted online at *www.birding.bc.ca*

A bald eagle surveys his domain

North to Nanaimo
'The Little Town that Did'

An hour's drive north from Victoria on the Malahat Highway (Highway 1) is the little coastal town of **Chemainus**. In the early 1980s, when the century-old sawmill closed and the town lay dying, a few artists began drawing larger-than-life murals on the exterior walls of buildings. Today, the town boasts Canada's largest outdoor art gallery, with 42 murals (*www.muraltown.com*) depicting the history of the Chemainus Valley. Subjects range from a 19th-century brigantine and Hong Hing's grocery store to portraits of First Nations people.

The town also has antique shops, art galleries, boutiques selling local crafts and souvenirs, and ice-cream parlours. A friendly place for lunch is The Willow Street Café, lodged in a 100-year-old heritage building. Try some quesadillas or daily special lunches on the spacious outdoor patio (*tel: (250) 246 2434; open: daily 8.30am–5.30pm*). In 2010, Chemainus introduced the 'Chemainus Dollar' (CH$) banknotes, accepted by Chemainus banks and some businesses, on par with Canadian currency – a unique souvenir (*see www.chemainusdollar.com*).

Wayside diversions

About 4km (3 miles) south of Nanaimo, right beside the road from Victoria, is tiny **Petroglyph Provincial**

Living walls in 'mural town', Chemainus

SNORKELLING WITH SALMON

If any life form can be called totemic for British Columbia, it's the salmon. For centuries, the many species (coho, chum, chinook, pink and sockeye) formed the basis of the First Nations diet and inspired their art. Today, its popularity continues not only as a delicious food and for sports fishing, but also as one of BC's newest adventures – snorkelling with salmon from late July to October. Destiny River Adventures, in Campbell River, provides wetsuits, guides and all the necessary snorkelling gear. Peeking at the fish in deep eddies, running the rapids or simply floating along with schools of salmon – and an occasional steelhead trout – all around is a true adrenalin high.
Destiny River Adventures.
Tel: (250) 287 4800, freephone (877) 923 7238; www.destinyriver.com

Park. A short stroll through the woods leads to a series of ancient First Nations rock carvings depicting people, birds, and the mythical seawolf. Visitors can make rubbings from replicas in the interpretive area.

'The Harbour City'

Nanaimo is best known as the 'Bathtub Capital of the World', referring to the annual July festival when dozens of tubbers challenge the often choppy waters to race 58km (36 miles) round from Nanaimo Harbour to Departure Bay Beach (*www.bathtubbing.com*). Also called 'The Harbour City', Nanaimo is a key link in the BC Ferries chain, with frequent regular sailings to and from Tsawwassen and Horseshoe Bay on the Lower Mainland.

A walking tour of the old town should include the **Nanaimo Museum**, Museum Way, Vancouver Island Conference Centre (*tel: (250) 753 1821; www.nanaimomuseum.ca*), which has exhibits explaining the arrival of the Spanish and discovery of coal, as well as Vancouver Island First Nations artefacts. The area highlight is **The Bastion**, on Front Street, built by the Hudson's Bay Company in 1853 to protect settlers from attack. This landmark is guarded by two of its original cannons; watch and listen in summer as the cannon is fired daily at noon.

Nanaimo is also famous for Nanaimo Bars, made of butter, icing sugar, a mixture of graham crackers and coconut, all wrapped in rich layers of chocolate.

Several typical restaurants such as The Blue Ginger (*1-5769 Turner Rd; tel: (250) 751 8238; www.thebluegingerrestaurant.com*), with Asian cuisine, and the Lighthouse Bistro (*50 Anchor Way; tel: (250) 754 3212; www.lighthouse-bistro.com*), specialise in local seafood. Mexican food at Gina's (*47 Skinner St; tel: (250) 753 5411; http://ginasmexicancafe.ca*) is a cheerful experience. Perched on a cliff top across from the law courts, this cosy little restaurant painted bright pink and blue is friendly, prices are reasonable, the clientele interesting and the sunset views superb. Nanaimo claims lots of retail space, so shoppers have lots of fun.

Parksville

When Captain Vancouver explored the area two centuries ago, he encountered only Coast Salish people. First settled in 1870, Parksville prospered with an economy based on forestry, tourism and farming. In recent years, development has been more spectacular, with large numbers of Canadians moving in to settle and to spend holidays enjoying the area's special attractions.

Beaches and sandcastles

The waters of the Strait of Georgia wash this coast. But whether the tide is in or out, there is always ample space on the beach for a family outing or a solitary stroll.

Low tide leaves great expanses of hard, clean sand several hundred metres wide. This is the time when beachcombers come to hunt for oysters and dig for clams, local residents walk their dogs, and visitors and their children wade in the shallow pools, fly kites and build sandcastles.

The month-long Parksville Beach Festival and Canadian Open Sand Sculpting Competition (*tel: (250) 951 2678; www.parksvillebeachfest.ca*) from mid-July to mid-August attract master builders from around the world who work quickly to complete their creations in the damp sand while the tide is out. The KidFest competition is for children (*tel: (250) 248 3252; www.kidfest.ca*).

At high tide, the hot summer sand warms the incoming water to a

Little Qualicum Falls, west of Coombs

comfortable swimming temperature. Parksville Beach claims the warmest outdoor swimming conditions in the province, with summer temperatures averaging 21°C (70°F). The shallow water provides an ideal water park where youngsters safely swim, splash about, and ride dinghies and tubes.

The beach is most memorable in the early morning, when the loons are calling, the seals are barking and, across the water, the distant, deep mauve mountains are emerging against the orange sky.

South of Parksville, more than 2km (1¼ miles) of sandy shore also beckon at **Rathtrevor Beach Provincial Park** (for reservations, *freephone: (800) 689 9025*), one of the most popular family camping spots on Vancouver Island.

There are also 5.5km (3¹/₂ miles) of hiking trails through parkland frequented by deer and rabbits, dozens of picnic tables and barbecue pits, children's play areas, a nature house, an amphitheatre and, in summer, nature interpretative programmes.

Special area attractions

As a change from the beach, **Paradise Adventure Golf** (*tel: (250) 248 6612; www.paradisefunpark.net*), centrally located in Parksville, has two 18-hole miniature courses with a fantasy setting which includes a pirate galleon, Victorian mansion, watermill, lighthouse and bright floral displays.

For history-lovers, **Craig Heritage Park and Museum** (*tel: (250) 248 6966; www.parksvillemuseum.ca*), 3km (2 miles) south of town, recalls the past with the 1912 Knox Church, the century-old French Creek post office, the McMillan log house, the Montrose school, a World War II-era fire station, and collections of late 19th-century clothing, old logging and farming equipment and early photographs of the area.

The Parksville Coast is a birdwatchers' paradise, with an abundance of bald eagles, blue herons, loons, harlequin ducks and trumpeter swans.

Of the 57 species found here, 19 are on the North American birdwatchers' list of most keenly sought birds. One of

these is the brent (brant) goose, about 20,000 of which stop here during March and April to feed on Pacific herring, which spawn offshore, on the way to their Alaska nesting grounds. The event is celebrated every March–April during the **Brant Wildlife Festival** (*tel: (604) 924 9771, freephone (866) 288 7878; www. brantfestival.bc.ca*). The area is also a mecca for anglers who come to fish the waters.

Places to eat and stay

Accommodation for visitors in the Parksville–Qualicum Beach–Coombs area includes 1,500 hotel and motel units ranging from rustic cabins to modern condominiums and luxury beach resorts, with an additional 2,000 camping and recreational vehicle (RV) sites.

A range of fast-food and family eating places can be found along the Island Highway. There are also more elegant gourmet restaurants, including the West Coast-inspired menu and BC wines at the Cedar Dining Room at Tigh-Na-Mara Seaside Spa Resort (*1115 Resort Dr, Parksville; freephone: (800) 663 7373; www.tigh-na-mara.com*).

For further information on the Parksville–Qualicum Beach–Coombs area, contact the Parksville & District Chamber of Commerce, PO Box 99, Parksville, BC V9P 2G3, or visit: *www.parksvillechamber.com*. The tourism Visitor Centre is south of Parksville (*1275 E Island Parkway; tel: (250) 248 3613*).

Qualicum Beach

A long beachside promenade begins near Parksville and heads north past hotels and seafood restaurants, with prime beachcombing when the tide is out. Qualicum Beach (*tel: (250) 752 9532; www.qualicum.bc.ca*) is a mecca for art-lovers, garden fans, birdwatchers and golfers. The Old School House (TOSH) (*tel: (250) 752 6133; www.theoldschoolhouse.org*) was renovated in the 1980s to house an art gallery with changing exhibits and seven studios to watch resident artists at work.

Gardens and the hanging baskets that colour village streets from spring to autumn are a source of pride. The area markets itself as 'Oceanside', and the Little Qualicum River Estuary to Nanoose Bay rates an Important Bird Area designation for more than 200 bird species, a draw for birdwatchers.

Good golf courses in the neighbourhood include Arrowsmith (18 holes; *tel: (250) 752 9727; www. golfarrowsmith.com*) north of town; Eaglecrest (18 holes; *tel: (250) 752 6311; www.eaglecrestgolfclub.ca*) just south of Qualicum Beach; Fairwinds (18 holes; *tel: (250) 468 7666; www.fairwinds.ca*) on the Nanoose Peninsula; Morningstar (18 holes; *freephone: (800) 567 1320; http://morningstargolf.com*) near the French Creek Marina; Pheasant Glen (18 holes; *tel: (250) 752 8786*) in town and Qualicum Beach Memorial (9 holes; *tel: (250) 752 6312; www. golfqualicum.ca*) on Crescent Road.

CATHEDRAL GROVE

About halfway along Highway 4, between Parksville and Port Alberni, stands Cathedral Grove, in MacMillan Provincial Park. Well-marked wilderness trails, carpeted with coniferous needles and cedar chips, wind beside lush ferns, hemlocks, cedars and a grove of 800-year-old Douglas fir trees, which survived a forest fire 300 years ago. The largest tree measures 3m (10ft) in diameter and 9m (30ft) in circumference, and stands 75m (246ft) tall. Interpretive signs explain the woodland cycle of growth and decay. Cathedral Grove's elegant, moss-draped trees create a sanctuary as awe-inspiring as any ancient religious building in Europe.

For more information, see *www.visitparksvillequalicumbeach.com*

Coombs

A ten-minute drive inland from Qualicum Beach, following Highway 4 to Port Alberni and Long Beach, is the tiny town of Coombs, instantly identifiable in summer by the goats that graze on the grass roof of the roadside Old Country Market (*www.oldcountrymarket.com*). The surrounding cluster of shops sells everything from candied apples and antler carvings to sportswear. The Coombs Country Bluegrass Festival held every summer at the rodeo grounds attracts country-and-western fans from all over the continent – probably a far cry from the demure, God-fearing colony intended when Salvation Army Commissioner Coombs led a dozen English families here to settle in 1910.

Nearby **Butterfly World & Gardens** (*Highway 4A; tel: (250) 248 7026; www.nature-world.com*) houses hundreds of exotic butterflies, representing 70 species, flying free in an enclosed tropical garden. Visitors can watch butterflies emerging from cocoons, flying, courting, sipping nectar, laying eggs or simply basking in the sunlight. Brush any butterflies off your shoulders before you leave.

Hillier's Sausage Factory (*tel: (250) 752 2390*), a few kilometres west just off the highway, is an essential stop for campers and almost anyone else,

since their European-style smoked meats are among the best in Canada.

Two provincial parks are also accessible from Coombs via Highway 4.

East of town, and some 16km (10 miles) south of the highway, is **Englishman River Falls Provincial Park**, with its impressive waterfall, gorges and pools set in forests of cedar, hemlock and fir trees.

Further west, on the way to Port Alberni, is **Little Qualicum Falls Provincial Park** with superb cataracts, pools and rocky chasms below kayak- and canoe-friendly Cameron Lake.

Vancouver's islands

The Old Country Market at Coombs, with resident 'roof goats'

Port Alberni

Port Alberni, a town of some 25,000 people, is the gateway to Vancouver Island's spectacular west coast and Pacific Rim National Park. About a three-hour drive from Victoria, it lies at the head of the long saltwater Alberni Inlet, midway along scenic Highway 4, which crosses the island's rugged interior. Named after the Spanish explorer Pedro de Alberni, who passed through the area two centuries ago, the town's lumber yards and mills, with only a few still in operation, are a reminder of a once-bustling lumber industry. To see how the lumber camps and sawmills worked, board harbourside, for a ride through town into the forest on the summertime Alberni Pacific 'Steam' Railway to the restored steam-powered operation at McLean Mill National Historic Site (*tel: (250) 723 1376; www.alberniheritage.com*).

Ferries provide a vital link between the islands

As the 'Salmon Capital of the World', Port Alberni attracts keen anglers year-round to fish the salmon-rich waters of Alberni Inlet and nearby Barkley Sound. The most experienced compete in contests for more than $48,000 in prizes during the annual Port Alberni Salmon Festival (*Clutesi Haven Marina; tel: (250) 720 3762; www.salmonfest.ca*), over Labour Day weekend.

The clock tower at Alberni Harbour Quay provides a panoramic view for miles around. Apart from the gift shops, art galleries, restaurants and boat companies running cruises and fishing charters, the lively quayside offers live entertainment, dining and people-watching while sipping a drink at one of the outdoor cafés.

Port Alberni is a good base for various outdoor activities in the area. Nearby **Mount Arrowsmith** (1,800m/5,906ft), which is snow-capped for most of the year, has a number of forest trails which are suitable for hiking in summer or skiing in winter (*for more information see www.albernivalleytourism.com*).

Sproat Lake

Only a 15-minute drive west out of Port Alberni via Highway 4, the community of Sproat Lake borders the vast freshwater lake and provincial park of the same name. This is the home base of the Martin Mars water bombers, the largest firefighting aircraft in the world, with tail-wing tips standing almost five storeys high. As they take off, these mammoth planes scoop up water from the lake to douse forest fires. Visitors are admitted to their land base unless operations prohibit access (*www.martinmars.com*). The aircraft are perhaps best seen from the deck of the Fish and Duck Pub (*tel: (250) 724 4331*) as they become silhouettes against the setting sun.

One of the most dramatic rainforest walks in the world is the short and little-known, but marked, trail from the water-bomber base to Sproat Lake Provincial Park. From the campsites, picnic tables and boat-launching ramp in the park, it is another ten-minute walk east along the lakeshore to a floating dock from which some of the most interesting ancient petroglyphs on

Della Falls, the highest in Canada

Vancouver Island can be viewed. Windsurfing, kayaking, canoeing, swimming and freshwater scuba diving are popular.

North of Sproat Lake, another intriguing place to visit is the **Robertson Creek Hatchery** (*tel: (250) 724 6521; www.pac.dfo-mpo.gc.ca; open: Mon–Fri 8.30am–3.30pm*) on the Stamp River, where millions of chinook, coho and steelhead salmon are bred annually. The best time to visit is in September or October when thousands of mature salmon return upstream after four years at sea and leap up a series of fish ladders in **Stamp River Provincial Park** (*tel: (250) 474 1336*) to spawn at their birthplace. Stamp River Falls also has a spawning ladders overlook where 40 million salmon pass annually.

Sproat Lake is also a good jumping-off point for an exciting two- to four-day excursion that includes a canoe or water-taxi ride along the entire length of nearby Great Central Lake, followed by a 16km (10-mile) hike along a trail to the spectacular **Della Falls**. Plunging 444m (1,457ft) in three magnificent cascades, the falls are Canada's highest.

MV *Frances Barkley*

Gracious but hard-working, the MV *Frances Barkley* (*tel: (250) 723 8313; freephone (800) 663 7192; www.ladyrosemarine.com*) is a sturdy 39m (128ft) long diesel packet freighter, launched in Stavanger, Norway in 1958. She has been ferrying freight and passengers since 1990, when she joined the venerable MV *Lady Rose* (now retired) in service from Port Alberni. She is licensed to carry 200 passengers and offers visitors memorable sailing adventures.

At 8am, a shrill blast announces the ship's departure from the Port Alberni Quay for the voyage westwards down Alberni Inlet to the Pacific Ocean. Passengers take breakfast or settle comfortably on the deck to enjoy the scenery. Dark forests rise sharply from the edges of the broad fjord. The ship sails along past China Creek and then ties up at the floating post office dock in Kildonan to unload mail and crates of goods. The next stops are at a couple of commercial fish farms, where groceries and pallets of fish food are delivered.

IF YOU GO

Pack sunscreen lotion, a warm sweater, a raincoat or windproof jacket, and wear practical shoes. The weather in Alberni Inlet may vary from hot sunshine to heavy rain and strong winds. Bring a camera and binoculars for watching birds and possibly seals and grey whales. Canoes and single and double kayaks, to enjoy the raw natural beauty of the Broken Islands, can be hired on a daily or weekly basis.

Remember that the ship is a working vessel, so dress accordingly.

For reservations and further information, *freephone: (800) 663 7192 Apr–Sept or tel: (250) 723 8313 Oct–Mar; www.ladyrosemarine.com*

Bald eagles circle overhead, hoping for leftovers. Then the *Frances Barkley* sails on to several isolated logging camps to unload mail and machinery parts.

The Broken Islands, part of the Pacific Rim National Park Reserve

Sailing adventures await along the waterfront

By noon on the year-round route the ship is docking at West Bamfield, where wooden boardwalks meander along the waterfront. As there is no road access here, water taxis cross the cove to East Bamfield, which is connected by a rough gravel logging road to Port Alberni. Accommodation is available for an overnight stay. Otherwise, the stopover time here may be 1–1½ hours.

In the summer (*Jun–mid-Sept*), the *Frances Barkley* takes visitors further north to the **Broken Islands Group**, in Barkley Sound. This cluster of about 100 small islands has several sheltered lagoons filled with seabirds and marine life that attract canoeists, kayakers and scuba divers. There is a stop at the Sechart Whaling Station, to drop off and pick up wilderness-lovers laden with kayaks and related equipment. The ship then stops for about an hour at the fishing village of Ucluelet, before heading back up Alberni Inlet. The arrival back at Port Alberni is usually between 5pm and 7pm.

BC's lumber industry

The Pacific Northwest rainforests, among the most luxuriant in the world, contain trees more than 1,000 years old. About half of BC – 60 million hectares (148 million acres) – is covered in forest, most of it on provincial land. To protect forest resources for the future, a Forest Practices Code was established in June 1995.

The BC government grants tree-farming licences to logging companies, who are required to take care of the forest, clean up any waste and plant new trees to replace those removed. Until the 1980s, only about one-third of the cleared land was being reforested. In 2009, less than 0.5 per cent of all BC trees were logged. Forestry companies have a government mandate to take better care of the forests, with selective cutting and more planting of species directly tailored for industry and bio-products, including fuel. Community forest management is a modern concept.

The lumber trade is still a major source of employment in BC

Logs may be transported by rail, road or sea

In 2009, 52,000 BC residents were directly employed in forestry – a number that had dropped sharply over several years.

The traditional lumberjack, in his long-sleeved checked shirt and heavy boots, axe in hand, has also disappeared. Instead chainsaws, bulldozers, tree stumpers, hydraulic barkers, loaders, sorters and other machinery are used. There are also heavy equipment operators, truck drivers, sawmill, pulp and paper-plant workers and tugboat captains.

After chainsaws fell trees, branches are removed, and cranes move logs to the roadside, where loading machines stack the logs on to trucks. The logs are then carried to a dumping ground and are sorted, measured and bundled. The biggest and best logs, such as those of the strong Douglas fir, go to plywood and other sawmills. Such smaller logs as western hemlock and balsam fir go to pulp and paper mills. Western red cedar, which is both weather- and rot-resistant, is often used for making roofing shales and shingles.

Pacific Rim National Park Reserve

No trip to Vancouver Island is complete without a visit to the wild and rugged Pacific Rim National Park Reserve on the western side of the island. Annual rainfall here averages 300cm (118in), so before setting out check *www.theweathernetwork.com/parksfx/CABC0663* for the weather forecast. The park is divided into three areas: from north to south, **Long Beach**, the **Broken Islands Group** and the **West Coast Trail**. More details at: *www.pc.gc.ca*

Long Beach

Long Beach is accessible by car along a winding mountain highway from Port Alberni. Solitary walkers love this broad 11km (7-mile) long stretch of surf-swept sand, rocky outcrops and tidal pools. Big drift-logs, bull kelp and brilliant sea anemones and starfish dot the sands, where lucky beachcombers can occasionally pick up glass fishing floats, watermarked like sterling silver to identify the villages in Japan from where they came. When summer surf is up at Incinerator Rock, it is fun to watch surfers catching the waves ashore.

Drop in at the Wickaninnish Restaurant in Pacific Rim National Park Reserve for a wickaccino, a signature espresso drink, or stay for dinner and admire the views of Vancouver Island's wild west coast. The restaurant also runs The Beachfront Café, a nice stop for a warming snack (call for dinner reservations; *tel: (250) 726 7706; www.wickaninnish.ca*).

WHALE WATCHING

Every spring from mid-March to mid-April, Pacific Rim National Park Reserve becomes a popular place for whale watching.

As their northbound migration reaches its peak, the 15m (49ft) long grey whales swim close to shore, often pausing to play in the coves and inlets along the coast.

Although whales are frequently sighted from rocky headlands along Long Beach, charter boat companies, such as **Jamie's Whaling Station** in Tofino (*tel: (250) 725 3919, freephone (800) 667 9913; www.jamies.com*) and **Remote Passages** (*tel: (250) 725 3330, freephone (800) 666 9833; www.remotepassages.com*), organise excursions.

The **Pacific Rim Whale Festival** at Tofino and Ucluelet in March (*tel: (250) 726 7798; www.pacificrimwhalefestival.com*) includes contests, artists, readings, excursions, tournament, concerts and plays. Programmes offer guided whale-spotting hikes, lectures and films.

The two towns nearby, **Ucluelet** and **Tofino**, offer a variety of restaurants and accommodation. Tofino (*www.tourismtofino.com*), surrounded by water on three sides, has several craft shops and art galleries. SoBo (*tel: (250) 725 2341*) serves meals with locally produced, and often wild, ingredients, and the Pacific Sands Beach Resort (*tel: (250) 725 3322, freephone (800) 565 2322; www.pacificsands.com*) has 77 spacious suites and villas overlooking Cox Bay.

West Coast Trail

Hardy hikers love the West Coast Trail, which meanders for 77km (48 miles) along an old telegraph route through wilderness rainforest, along sandstone cliffs and across slippery boardwalks in the southern part of Pacific Rim National Park Reserve. This rugged coastline was known as the graveyard of the Pacific for all the ships which sank off its shores.

The hike, which takes about a week to complete, is not for the faint-hearted. About a quarter of the hikers who set out do not manage to finish. But those who challenge this treacherous trail, accessible only from May to September and to just 60 permitted hikers daily, are rewarded with the smell of the salty sea air; breathtaking views of undisturbed shoreline; occasional sightings of pods of whales and pudgy sea lions, and seabirds such as pigeon guillemots, marbled murrelets and pelagic cormorants; **Tsusiat Falls**, where several cascades have created super swimming holes near the shore; and a campfire under the stars.

The trail (information and reservations: tel: (250) 647 5434 or (250) 728 3234) runs from Port Renfrew to Bamfield, or vice versa. Reservations are required and can be made Jun 15–Sept 15, or take a chance for a standby slot.

The indented coastline at Tofino, in Pacific Rim National Park Reserve

Tour: Sunshine Circle

For visitors wanting to make the most of a two-week holiday in BC coastal country, this 2–4-day driving circuit is ideal. It includes four ferry rides (though the queues can be horrendous in summer) and takes in the Sunshine Coast and east Vancouver Island (www.sunshinecoastcanada.com). Begin at Horseshoe Bay, a 30-minute drive northwest from downtown Vancouver, where BC Ferries (tel: (888) 223 3779; www.bcferries.com) sail the 16km (10 miles) across Howe Sound from Horseshoe Bay to Langdale eight times a day.

1 Gibsons

From Langdale, a 3km (2-mile) long road winds west through forests and farmland along a craggy coastline to Gibsons, the gateway to the Sunshine Coast. Visitors like to tour Molly's Reach, the set where the television series *The Beachcombers*, the longest-running show in Canada, was filmed. Other options include a half-hour stroll along the sea walk to a stone cairn marking the spot where Captain Vancouver landed two centuries ago, and studying the First Nations displays and pioneer and natural history at the Sunshine Coast Museum. West of Gibsons, just off the main road, are good beaches and hiking trails. Nearby Roberts Creek, a community of artists and artisans, has a camping site right on the water's edge.

2 Sechelt

About 14km (8¾ miles) northwest of Gibsons stands Sechelt, the cultural centre of the Sunshine Coast. Abundant and colourful marine life draws scuba divers.

Seafood is served at the Wharf Restaurants on Davis Bay and at the Blue Heron (*http://blueheronrestaurant.ca*). Sechelt First Nations people, Canada's first self-governing aboriginal group, are renowned for fine carvings and woven cedar baskets; visit the Tems Swiya Museum.

3 Skookumchuk Narrows Provincial Park

About 35km (25 miles) north on the road from Sechelt is Egmont. From here, an hour's hiking leads to lookouts above the Skookumchuk Narrows, where strong tides (highest at the summer and winter solstices) from three inlets rush at speeds of up to 15 knots through the spectacular rock-strewn passage. A 50-minute ferry connects nearby Earls Cove with Saltery Bay across Jervis Inlet, where bald eagles fly overhead and killer whales, seals and sea lions compete for slow salmon. Divers can see the bronze mermaid anchored 20m (65ft) down in Mermaid Cove, part of Saltery Bay Provincial Park.

4 Powell River

The next town, Powell River, offers the best salt- and freshwater fishing in Canada. Hiking, mountain biking climbing Eldred River Valley cliffs, coastal canoeing or kayaking and scuba diving here are for the intrepid. See *www.discoverpowellriver.com*

5 Comox

Four ferries sail daily from Powell River to Comox (dock at Little River) on Vancouver Island, an 80-minute cruise west. Once known for coal mining, now fishing, forestry, farming and tourism

sustain the Comox Valley. Visitors come for the sandy beaches, the local handicrafts and Snowbirds aerial spring training in April. The Filberg Heritage Lodge and Park (*www.filberg.com*) is a good place to enjoy afternoon tea followed by a stroll in the gardens. See *www.discovercomoxvalley.com*

6 Courtenay

In the adjacent town of Courtenay, the Courtenay and District Museum and Palaeontology Centre (*www. courtenaymuseum.ca*) boasts local fossil finds, dolls and First Nations artefacts. *Allow about two hours for the winding road following the coast south to Nanaimo, and two hours more to sail back to Horseshoe Bay by ferry.*

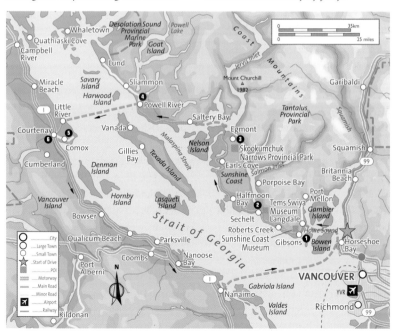

Getting away from it all

A great quadrangle stretching between the 49th and 60th parallels, Canada's westernmost province brims with opportunities for relaxation, recreation and adventure. Four times the size of Great Britain, BC's great outdoors extends between mountains and valleys, rivers and lakes, rainforests and deserts, coastlines and islands. Haida Gwaii, to the northwest, is attractive to kayakers, to birdwatchers and to lovers of aboriginal art.

The Pacific Ocean washes the shores of BC's main islands, Vancouver Island and Haida Gwaii (Queen Charlotte Islands). On Vancouver Island, Pacific Rim National Park Reserve lures whale-watchers and other naturalists to wild beaches. Inland hikers explore the meadows of Forbidden Plateau and Strathcona Provincial Park and the first-growth rainforest in Cathedral Grove and the Carmanah Valley. East of Vancouver, the terrain opens into the Okanagan Valley, where wineries flank dude ranches and bird sanctuaries. The valley also has extensive apple, cherry and peach orchards. Further east, beyond the good hiking terrain of the Kootenays, stand the majestic **Rocky Mountains**, a mere 65 million years old, flanking the much older **Purcell Mountains**. The Rockies and Purcells became neighbours during the age of the dinosaurs. The Burgess Shale site in **Yoho National Park** contains fossils from an ancient sea.

The high interior plateau of the Cariboo Chilcotin attracts equestrians, some of whom head out from the Sundance Guest Ranch (*www.sundanceguestranch.com*) on horseback to explore scenic trails, mountain meadows and river valleys. Canadian River Expeditions (*www.nahanni.com*) offers an 11-day 'Best of British Columbia Whitewater Rafting' circuit, which includes a boat cruise up the coast to Bute Inlet; a floatplane flight over the Homatho Icefield to turquoise Chilko Lake, and a day of fishing and hiking; an exciting raft trip along the Chilko, Chilcotin and Fraser Rivers to the town of **Lillooet**; and a scenic return to Vancouver.

North of the Cariboo Chilcotin stretches dramatic landscape and weather. Stewart, Canada's most northerly ice-free port, has recorded up to 27m (89ft) of snowfall in one year. Winter lures visitors to explore the region by dog sledge and skidoo and on Nordic skis, while summer elsewhere in BC offers boating on **Atlin Lake**, rafting through icebergs on the great

Tatshenshini River, and big game and wildlife-spotting in Spatsizi Plateau Wilderness Provincial Park.

Beaches

BC's 27,000km (16,780-mile) coastline, dotted with 6,500 islands, boasts lots of beaches, most suitable for sunning, swimming and beachcombing in summer. Vancouver Island is surrounded by beaches, and the Sunshine Coast (*www.sunshinecoastcanada.com*) sports its share, too.

One of the province's most treasured beaches is fairly remote. Travel to the end of Highway 101 to Lund, north of Powell River on the Sunshine Coast, and take the 15-minute Lund water-taxi ride (*tel: (604) 483 9749*) to **Savary Island**. Ironically, the most subdivided real estate in Canada, this crescent-shaped gem is ringed with long beaches, reminiscent of the South Pacific. A warm current mingles with the tides to produce summer waters reaching 22°C (72°F). When Captain Vancouver landed here in 1792, after a long voyage through the South Seas, he admired this island for 'beauty such as we have seldom enjoyed'. The pace of life has not changed much since. The four dozen permanent residents share Savary with many visitors, especially in summer. They come for the beautiful beaches, the warm waters and the many plants that normally grow much further south.

Near the government wharf, along 'Dough Row', windsurfers skim along with the breeze. Further away from human habitation, beachcombers find a variety of seashells, multicoloured rocks, and perfectly preserved sand dollars. Following the beaches around the island for about 29km (18 miles) is a full day's walk. A sign nearby marks the trail to North America's largest arbutus tree. It takes four adults, arms stretched and touching at the fingertips, to circle the tree's girth.

Visitors who want to linger longer will find a few rental cottages and B&Bs, but no formal campsites. Overnighters who insist on sleeping on the beach are warned to watch for changing tides.

Getting away from it all

A pristine and deserted beach, one of many on BC's extensive coastline

Boating

More than 250,000 BC households have boats. With so many waterways, boating seems as natural as driving. The choices are many and varied, ranging from a simple sunset dinner cruise around English Bay or a passive ride aboard a big BC ferry, to running the rapids of the mighty Fraser River or fishing offshore with whales, sea lions and cormorants for company.

Atlin Lake

For a boating adventure in the true north, head for Atlin, which lies near the BC/Yukon border. Atlin Lake, which is 100km (62 miles) long, is the place to be in midsummer when the sun rises at 4.30am and sets at 11.15pm, leaving enough light to take midnight photos. Kayakers and canoeists can also go ashore to hike, look for mountain goats, bathe in hot springs and admire alpine scenery.

The best way to get there is to fly to Whitehorse in the Yukon, and rent a car or catch the Atlin Express or Art Centre bus for the two to three-hour ride south to Atlin. From there, access is by boat or air.

The Bowron Lakes Circuit

The quietest and most relaxing boating adventure may be the Bowron Lakes circuit, named one of the top ten canoe trips in the world by *Outside Magazine*. Deep in the heart of the Cariboo Mountains west of the Rockies, this rectangular chain of lakes and connecting waterways is set within a 149,207-hectare (368,685-acre) wilderness park. Along the 116km (72-mile) route, the placid blue waters reflect glacier-streaked mountains rising to 2,100m (6,890ft). The region is home to many birds and wildlife such as moose, grizzly bears, coyotes and beavers. The 6–10-day circuit, with a shorter section that can be canoed in 1–3 days, can be enjoyed from June to October, although June seems to be the best month for seeing both birds and other wildlife. Canoeist numbers are limited; to make reservations *tel: (519) 826 6850, freephone (800) 689 9025; http://www.env.gov.bc.ca/bcparks/ explore/parkpgs/bowron_lk/can_broch. pdf.* **Pathways Tours** (*tel: (604) 514 8024, freephone (800) 924 2944; www.bowronlakes.com*) organises canoeing tours through the Bowron Lakes for novice paddlers.

Desolation Sound

Lund, on the Sunshine Coast (*see p127* for how to get there), and Campbell River, on eastern Vancouver Island, are good starting points for Desolation Sound, 31km (19 miles) north of Powell River. One of BC's largest provincial marine parks, Desolation Sound offers protected warm waters backed by coastal mountains. Native pictographs and coastal lakes make trips ashore interesting, and the waters provide fresh oysters and salmon for dinner.

The Gulf Islands

Sailing the sheltered waters of the Gulf Islands is great fun. But watch for 'deadheads', mostly submerged waterlogged tree trunks which have escaped from log booms, which could grind your vessel to an untimely halt. Some boat rental companies offer weekend flotilla charters, in which a group of boats sails in the company of a mother ship skippered by a certified instructor. The instructor does the navigating, thus enabling out-of-towners to explore unknown waters with ease. Courses are also offered in basic coastal cruising, coastal navigation, advanced sailing, celestial navigation and offshore sailing.

Okanagan Lake

Okanagan Lake is located in the Okanagan Valley of BC. The freshwater lake is clear, 150km (93 miles) long and 232m (761ft) deep. It is surrounded by mountains and several communities, the largest being Kelowna, in a region known for vineyards and wineries.

Okanagan Lake has become a popular venue for waterskiing, boating, houseboating and sunbathing at the many surrounding beaches.

It is also home to the Ogopogo, a legend in the Okanagan; many people attempt to capture this 'friendly serpent' on film.

Princess Louisa Inlet

Jervis Inlet, further south on the Sunshine Coast, leads to Princess Louisa Inlet, one of the most scenic fjords in the world. Bordered by craggy granite cliffs streaked with waterfalls and capped with evergreens, the fiord is home to many sea mammals and birds. Erle Stanley Gardner said, 'There is no use in describing that inlet. Perhaps an atheist could view it and remain an atheist, but I doubt it.' On top of the gorge is a marine park, crowned by the 40m (131ft) high Chatterbox Falls.

Shuswap Lake

For a different boating holiday, head for the interior town of **Sicamous**, on the Trans-Canada Highway west of Revelstoke. Holidaymakers can rent a houseboat, complete with a hot tub on the deck, take the wheel, and head out to tie up at one of Shuswap Lake's beaches. The houseboats are simple to manoeuvre and great fun for families. Houseboaters can swim, fish and explore the area onshore from their floating home.

For information *see www.shuswap.bc.ca*

In BC, boating is almost as popular as driving

If you go

Request the *BC Outdoor Adventure Guide* brochures from Tourism BC (*www.hellobc.com*), or any BC Visitor CentreCall Tourism Yukon (*tel: (800) 661 0494; http://travelyukon.com*) for information on trips to and on Atlin Lake.

Running the rapids

Suddenly a menacing sound rumbles ahead. There is no turning back now. 'Hang on tight!' shouts the boatman. The big rubber raft careens through the foaming rapids. White water slams the pontoons, then gracefully sprays up and falls, and the raft plunges with the flow downstream to calmer waters.

This is rapid-running, but on such chauffeured expeditions, skilled rapid-runners man the oars. The rafts are not easy to capsize, but passengers wear life jackets, just in case. In rough water, the

---

SIMON FRASER

Simon Fraser was an American-born fur trader and explorer for the North West Company. He was also one of the great river-runners of the 19th century.

In 1808, against the advice of the native Indians, he led an expedition in birch-bark canoes down a river he believed to be the Columbia. He was mistaken, and that fast river of many rapids and deep gorges now bears his name.

At Hell's Gate, Fraser wrote: 'It is so wild that I cannot find words to describe our situation at times … a desperate undertaking!'

His persistent and perilous journey changed the map of the continent.

---

raft may buck and leap like a Wild West bronco. River-running is not always a dry experience, so keep cameras in waterproof bags.

River-running is more than just navigating rivers. Most trips allow time for hikes ashore and a cooling swim in the river. On longer trips, the boatmen may become chefs and grill salmon steaks or hamburgers over an open fire, while the aroma of freshly brewed coffee fills the air. Often a happy evening can be spent around a campfire chatting with new-found friends, with time left over to gaze at the moon and stars before settling in for the night.

Chilko River

An exciting four–six-day rafting trip follows the Chilko River. The run is gentle from Chilko Lake to Cataract Canyon, where sets of Class III–V rapids await the rafter. The last stretch runs from the Taseko River junction to the Chilcotin River junction.

Creston Valley

A gentler journey is the one- to three-day canoe trip through the Creston Valley (*www.crestonvalley.com*). Paddlers start at the Canada/US border on Highway 21 and go north with the flow to Kootenay Lake. Protected marshlands make for safe canoeing.

More than 250 species of birds inhabit or visit the valley, and the area between Creston and Nelson is home to 140 pairs of osprey, one of the largest osprey nesting sites in the world.

Rafters need skill and courage to brave the rapids

Contact the Creston Valley Wildlife Management Area (*tel: (250) 402 6908; www.crestonwildlife.ca*) for more canoeing information.

The mighty Fraser River

Several powerful rivers surge through BC, carrying such aboriginal names as Chilko and Chehalis (meaning 'where the chest of a canoe grounds on a sandbar'), and honouring such early explorers as David Thompson and Simon Fraser. But the Fraser River is the greatest of them all.

Rising as a trickle in the southeast corner of Mount Robson Provincial Park in the Rockies, the Fraser travels 1,375km (855 miles) southwest to empty into the Pacific. From Mount Robson, the river flows fast and pristine to Quesnel. There are rapids at Scuzzy

Rock, China Bar and **Hell's Gate** – appropriately named, for here the mighty Fraser churns through a narrow, glacially carved 34m (112ft) wide gorge. As the raft runs from Boston Bar for 42km (26 miles) down to Yale, the boatman usually gives a running commentary on the mining history of the area.

For a calmer Fraser River trip, boaters start at Hope and wend their way past New Westminster to the Oak Street Bridge in Vancouver, where urban development is under way on all sides.

Chilliwack River Rafting Adventures
Freephone: (800) 410 7238; www.chilliwackriverrafting.com
Fraser River Raft Expeditions Ltd
Tel: (800) 363 7238; www.fraserraft.com

Hyak Wilderness Adventures
Freephone: (800) 663 7238;
www.hyak.com
Kumsheen Raft Adventures
Freephone: (800) 663 6667;
www.kumsheen.com
Whistler River Adventures
Tel: (604) 932 3532,
freephone (888) 932 3532;
www.whistlerriver.com

Provincial parks

There are more than 900 provincial parks in BC, encompassing glaciers, grasslands, rainforests, rivers, lakes, dormant volcanoes, mountains, islands, fjords and beaches. There are over 6,000km (3,729 miles) of hiking trails, and more than 90 parks with good canoeing and hiking, some with good fishing and some with boat launches. More than 11,000 pitches in 340 campsites are scattered throughout the parks. Some have interpretive programmes, so visitors can hear talks about flora and fauna and star-gaze with astronomers. Parks and protected lands cover more than 14 per cent of BC, and BC Provincial Parks are, after Parks Canada (Canada's national parks), the second-largest parks system in the country. For more information, see BC Parks: *www.env.gov.bc.ca/bcparks*

Mount Robson Provincial Park

A favourite with many adventurers, Mount Robson Provincial Park contains the highest peak (3,954m/ 12,972ft) in the Canadian Rockies, the headwaters of the Fraser River and spectacular scenery. From June to September, visitors admire more than 50 species of alpine flowers, 182 species of birds (including golden eagles), grizzly bears, caribou, mountain goats and hoary marmots. Robson Helimagic (*freephone: (877) 454 4700; www.robsonhelimagic.com*) flies over the park, with heli-hiking nearby. The mountain base nestles in a rain shadow surrounded by flowering meadows and snowy peaks. The 23km (14-mile) Berg Lake Trail is one of the Rockies' most popular wilderness trails; a reservation is required for camping.

Pure water flows in glacier-fed streams. Hikers bathe downstream in natural pools and waterfalls, and spend about six hours each day exploring the wilderness. The Northern Lights occasionally brighten the dark sky.

Strathcona Provincial Park

BC's oldest park boasts six of the seven highest peaks on Vancouver Island, along with the Comox Glacier, the island's last remaining ice field, thus earning it the nickname 'Little Switzerland'. Although Strathcona is truly a wilderness park, day-trippers take the half-hour drive west from Courtenay in the Comox Valley in summer to enjoy the alpine flowers and hike the Forbidden Plateau.

Available accommodation includes campsites at Buttle Lake and Ralph River, and the Strathcona Park Lodge (*tel: (250) 286 3122;*

www.strathcona.bc.ca), on the lake just outside the park. The lodge's superb outdoor education centre offers wilderness leadership, rock climbing, mountaineering, white-water canoeing, kayaking and wildlife photography. Experienced hikers enjoy the Flower Ridge, Elk River and Marble Meadows Trails radiating out from Buttle Lake, as well as the challenge of scaling the 2,200m (7,218ft) Golden Hinde. **Della Falls**, Canada's highest at 444m (1,457ft), are located in the southern part of the park. Visitors take a watertaxi from the Ark Resort (*tel: (250) 723 2657; www.arkresort.com*) near Port Alberni up Great Central Lake and then hike 16km (10 miles) to the falls.

Tweedsmuir Provincial Park

This is one of BC's largest parks. Many overseas visitors rent campers in Vancouver, drive north to Williams Lake on the Cariboo Highway (97), and then west on the Freedom Highway (20) to Bella Coola. This route runs through Tweedsmuir (South) Provincial Park. Hair-raising switchbacks down The Hill, as it is known, losing 1,219m (4,000ft) in 16km (10 miles) before entering the **Atnarko River Valley**, lead to a good location for day hikes into the Rainbow Mountains.

The Rainbow Mountain Outfitting (*tel: (250) 742 3539; www. rainbowadventuresbc.com*) of Anahim Lake, guides in these parts for three generations, come highly recommended

for week-long horseback outings during July and August. The **Hunlen Lakes** area, which provides excellent canoeing, is where the pioneer settler Ralph Edwards helped save trumpeter swans from extinction during the 1950s. Ralph's son John runs the Hunlen Wilderness Camp.

Wells Gray Provincial Park

Considered one of BC's finest parks, it is located just north of Clearwater, a five-hour drive north from Vancouver on Highway 5. The park offers great hiking in summer and hut-to-hut skiing in winter. Clearwater Lake is easily accessible and offers good beaches and good fishing. In winter, the 142m (466ft) Helmcken Falls freeze into a 20-storey ice cone, broader at the base than a football field. Helmcken Falls Lodge (*tel: (250) 674 3657; www.helmckenfalls.com*) was originally built as a hunting lodge at the entrance to the park. Visitors love it as a base for hiking, canoeing, backpacking, horse riding, mountaineering, glacier exploration and fishing.

Waterfalls appear beside the road, here between Ucluelet and Tofino

The iron horse

The history of the railway in Canada is the history of the development of this sprawling, rugged land. The Canadian Pacific Railway (CPR) was founded in 1881 and it took 54 months to complete. The last spike was driven in Craigellachie, BC, in 1885. The line connects Montreal with Port Moody, BC, a distance of 4,627km (2,876 miles).

Where the iron horse ambled, settlers and prosperity usually followed. The first scheduled passenger train arrived in Vancouver in 1887. The arrival of the railway energised the economy of the Pacific Northwest, bringing large numbers of Canadians and Europeans west. The population of Vancouver mushroomed from 900 to 8,000 within five years, and the Canadian Pacific Railway (*www.cprheritage.com*) became the city's largest employer.

The CPR built the first Hotel Vancouver, bought and sold land, operated sternwheelers on BC rivers and ran steamships across the Pacific Ocean. Freight trains running across the country encouraged the exploitation of natural resources. BC products such as fur, coal, timber, gold and fish suddenly found accessible markets.

The transcontinental train service has been curtailed in recent years, since cars and trucks, along with aircraft and helicopters, have diminished passenger demand. Most British Columbians now drive or fly to get from one place to another, but holidaymakers love the romance and the rattle of the rails, the gentle pace, and the friendliness of the conductors and other passengers from all over the world.

Thundering past snow-capped mountains

CPR tracks run through some remarkable scenery

Yet the scenery remains the greatest attraction. Early CPR President Cornelius Van Horne commented in 1895, 'Since we cannot export the scenery, we shall have to import the tourists.'

Rail travellers love the stillness and splendour of the unfolding wilderness panorama of mountains, canyons, lakes, rivers, streams, forests and rolling ranchlands, and glimpses of such elusive wildlife as deer, elk, moose, bighorn sheep and bear. They love the dramatic spiral tunnels near Kicking Horse Pass; the geography lesson; whistle stops at remote towns and villages; and the sense of pioneer adventure.

For information on scenic rail tours across Canada, see:
www.royalcanadianpacific.com,
www.viarail.ca,
www.rockymountaineer.com

Getting away from it all

Riding the rails

Rail travel is so much a part of BC's history that it's hard to have a complete BC experience without travelling on a train. Rocky Mountaineer's Whistler Sea to Sky Climb™ is a three-hour rail trip along the sea-to-sky route that follows the coastline along Howe Sound from Vancouver to Whistler.

The Rocky Mountaineer ride through British Columbia to the Rockies has been dubbed one of the most spectacular rail tours in the world. Passengers return again and again to enjoy the dramatic journey. Although the trip could be done in a day, the Rocky Mountaineer takes two days with an overnight stop so that passengers can soak in the maximum eye-popping views during daylight hours. On the first day, the biggest 'wows' come through the **Fraser Canyon**; on the second day, it's **Mount Robson** as the train approaches the Rockies. On-board entertainment is part of the ride, but the best bit is the running commentary by staff members, who pride themselves on knowing absolutely everything and delivering their facts with humour and drama. During the journey, lush rainforests are punctuated by deep canyons and raging waterfalls. There are lakes and forests, painted deserts, dramatic bridges high above rivers, tunnels, glaciers and soaring mountain peaks and local cuisine served against the panoramic mountain and coastal scenery.

Rocky Mountaineer has several routes: Journey through the Clouds™, from Vancouver to Kamloops and Jasper; First Passage to the West™, from Vancouver to Kamloops, Banff and Calgary; and Rainforest to Gold Rush™ (which can be an add-on to the Whistler Sea to Sky Climb™), with boarding in Whistler to go north into the Fraser River Cariboo Gold Rush region as far as Quesnel, then east to Jasper (*tel: (877) 460 3200; www.rockymountaineer.com*).

Vancouver is also the Western terminus for VIA Rail's Canadian, a continuous trip from the coast to Toronto, taking in the full panorama of Canada's distinct geographic changes. Seeing the country with VIA is a once-in-a-lifetime dream for many visitors. Another VIA service follows a northerly route across the middle of the province from Prince Rupert to Jasper.

Riding the trails

Horse riding is an easy and pleasant way to explore BC outdoors. Riding appeals to almost everyone: the views can be marvellous, the pace therapeutic and the environmental impact minimal. Because the animals carry the gear, horseback holidays have extra appeal for families with young children, who might find arduous hikes overwhelming. Most BC outfitters and dude ranchers use placid quarter horses and Arabian stock for trekking. They have comfortable gaits and respond to neck-reining, which allows one hand free to hang on to the saddle horn.

In the Lower Mainland, latent cowpokes can canter in Golden Ears Provincial Park with professional guide riders out of Maple Ridge for a day trek to Alouette Lake, where they can hitch their horses to a tree and go for a swim. Several hundred kilometres of trails in **Manning Provincial Park** are ideal for rambling through Canada's mountainous west. Late summer or autumn is a good season to ride, as the insects retreat and the autumn leaves turn bright red, rust and yellow. In mid-September at Manning, the alpine larch trees on Frosty Mountain turn a deep gold before dropping their deciduous needles.

North of Vancouver, from **Williams Lake** (*www.williamslake.ca*), riders can head west to **Tatlayoko Lake** in the Chilcotin for week-long journeys to see ice caves, fossil beds and meadows where grizzly bears forage in the Potato Mountain Coast Range.

East of Williams Lake, riders can overnight at Helmcken Falls Lodge (*tel: (250) 674 3657; www.helmckenfalls.com*) near Clearwater and ride lodge horses along the trails of Wells Gray Park.

For unusual trekking, try remote **Mount Edziza Provincial Park** (contact the Stikine District Office, *tel: (250) 771 4591*). Tahltan First Nations guides introduce riders to moonscapes of cinder cones and mountains of shale, occasionally pockmarked by hungry grizzlies hunting gophers. Any saddle sores suffered during the long trek may be soothed by hellebore root, which the guide boils up in an old tin can.

Getting away from it all

Horse riding is a great way to explore BC

The Rockies

This mountainous region of outstanding scenic splendour stretches northwest for 1,400km (870 miles) along the BC–Alberta border. It is bounded on the east by vast prairies and on the west by the Rocky Mountain Trench, one of the longest valleys in the world. Most of the Rocky Mountains are in Alberta. For much of their length, they form the Continental Divide separating Canada's east- and west-flowing rivers.

Mount Robson, the highest peak, rises 3,954m (12,972ft) skyward, while **Mount Assiniboine**, the Matterhorn of Canada, is a breathtaking 3,618m (11,870ft) tusk of layered rock carved into a pyramid shape by glacial cirques.

The Rockies were created about 65 million years ago, when the land uplifted and broke along great fault lines, forcing the rock to fold and buckle. During the last Ice Age, about 12,000 years ago, glaciers completed this natural sculpting process.

The Kootenay First Nations have lived here for 10,000 years. As hunters and gatherers, they knew all the secret passes through the mountains. When the explorer and fur trader David Thompson eventually struggled through Howes Pass in 1807, the Kootenays nicknamed him 'Star Man'.

Although other explorers and traders, prospectors, missionaries and homesteaders (pioneer farmers) followed, few settled. The discovery of gold at Wild Horse Creek in 1863 brought a surge of 5,000 souls, but when the gold was gone only about 20 families remained. Two decades later, the Northwest Mounted Police established a detachment here.

Today, the Kootenay Rockies area is a haven for the adventure tourist in passionate pursuit of the peaks and outdoor action. The air is fresh, the waters clear and the scenery awesome. From such guest ranches as Beaverfoot and Bull River (*http://bullriver.bcresorts. com*), visitors can canter around the countryside all day and return to find freshly caught rainbow trout sizzling on the grill. Others may prefer to hike over alpine meadows, play golf or paddle, sail, windsurf or waterski on emerald lakes. Or they may savour the silvery cascades of Laughing Falls, or soak in warmer water at the Radium or Fairmont hot springs.

Wildlife watchers, especially at dawn and dusk, may spot moose, deer, elk, mountain goat, bear, lynx, coyote and marmot. Winter resorts offer Nordic and alpine skiing, while heli-skiing (helicopter skiing) in the Bugaboo area is an experience of a lifetime.

Fort Steele

At this fine historic heritage town, the gold-mining past is vividly present in over 60 reconstructed buildings. Highlights include ice-cream making, steam-train and horse-drawn wagon rides, gold panning, Victorian vaudeville at the Wild Horse Theatre and workers costumed as blacksmiths, carpenters, quilters, weavers and residents.

The town is 16km (10 miles) northeast of Cranbrook. Tel: (250) 426 7352, 24-hour hotline; www.fortsteele.ca. Open: daily dawn–dusk. Admission charge.

Kimberley

Canada's highest city at 1,117m (3,665ft), Kimberley is nicknamed the 'Bavarian City of the Rockies'. The red-brick pedestrian Platzl holds the world's largest operating cuckoo clock. Bavarian-style buildings sport dark wood panelling, floral decorations and window boxes filled with red geraniums. European delis and restaurants serve such German specialities as Weisswurst, Spetzle and Strudel. Kimberley has been a zinc-, silver- and lead-mining town since the 1890s. The Kimberley Underground Mining Railway tour carries visitors in an old mining car through a tunnel to a hands-on experience with mining equipment.
For information tel: (250) 427 3666, freephone (866) 913 3666; www.kimberleychamber.ca

Kootenay National Park

Here, a half-hour hike through moss-carpeted forest leads to the Paint Pots, ponds stained red, orange and yellow by iron oxide, which the Kootenay First Nations used for body and rock painting.
Located south of Yoho National Park. Open: year-round. Tel: (250) 347 9505.

Yoho National Park

With 28 peaks more than 3,000m (9,843ft) high, all layered with rock, blue ice and snow, this park offers such varied sights as the Takakkaw Falls, the spiral railway tunnels leading up to Kicking Horse Pass and the Burgess Shale fossil beds, which include remains of 120 species, dating as far back as 530 million years.
Located just west of the Continental Divide and Banff National Park. Open: year-round. Tel: (250) 343 6783.

Banff and Jasper National Parks (Alberta)

Canada's oldest national park, Banff was established in 1885 after hot springs were seen gushing from the side of Sulphur Mountain. The main resort towns are Banff, named after Banffshire in Scotland, and Lake Louise, located north of Banff on the Continental Divide. Jasper National Park, the largest designated parkland in the Rocky Mountains, lies north of Banff and west of Edmonton. Scenic highlights include **Mount Edith Cavell** and **Maligne Lake**, a large and beautiful remnant of a retreating glacier. The Columbia Icefield, a glacier that has not yet retreated, is about an hour's drive south. Consult The Mountain Guide for the most detailed, current information on all six Canadian Rockies National Parks, also including Glacier and Mount Revelstoke, in British Columbia:
www.pc.gc.ca

For further information, contact Kootenay Rockies Tourism, tel: (250) 427 4838; www.kootenayrockies.com

Shopping

Western Canadians have been shopping in Vancouver ever since the Oppenheimer brothers began outfitting prospectors and homesteaders more than a century ago. The range of goods has, of course, expanded far beyond the dreams of those early settlers, and sturdy outdoor clothing is as much a fashion item as a necessity these days.

The high standard of living and high expectations of its citizens have made Vancouver a wonderful place to shop – and prices are often lower than in Europe. There are shops everywhere, from the heritage areas of Gastown to the modern, underground Pacific Centre mall; from colourful markets to trendy designer boutiques.

In addition to all the usual shopping mall and high-street retailers, there are specialist stores for just about everything: items for left-handed people, clothes for short or tall people, shoes for big feet, pewterware, cigars, artistic chocolates, etc. The eclectic range of goods is also broadened by the cultures of immigrant populations.

Robson Street is the hub of it all – the most popular strolling street in Vancouver – where people meet and greet, gaze at store windows filled with clothes and curios from around the globe, and linger in the cafés and restaurants to watch the world go by.

Robson Square is the focal point for trendy shopping on Robson Street. The other main shopping streets are Water Street in Gastown, Pender Street in Chinatown and South Granville Street for art, antiques and carpets.

Arts and crafts

Canoe Pass Gallery
The work of gifted Canadian Native artists is on display in this heritage-village gallery, including masks, carvings, prints, jewellery and sculpture.
3866 Bayview St, Steveston.
Tel: (604) 272 0095; www.canoepass.com

Coastal Peoples Fine Arts Gallery
Native artwork, including gold and silver jewellery, masks, totem poles, paintings, prints and Inuit sculptures.
1024 Mainland St, Yaletown.
Tel: (604) 685 9298;
www.coastalpeoples.com

Crafthouse
The gallery of the Crafts Association of British Columbia, with items chosen to

represent a spirit of exploration and a tradition of quality.

1386 Cartwright St, Granville Island.
Tel: (604) 687 6511;
www.craftcouncil.bc.ca

Hill's Native Art

An enormous – and probably the largest – selection of Northwest Coast First Nations art- and craftwork in BC.

165 Water St, Gastown.
Tel: (866) 685 5422. Also at 1008 Government St, Victoria (tel: (250) 385 3911); 76 Bastion St, Nanaimo (tel: (250) 755 7873); and at 5209 TransCanada Highway, Kosilah (tel: (250) 746 6731);
www.hillsnativeart.com

Inuit Gallery

Opposite the Gastown Steam Clock is one of the most elegant and spacious First Nations art galleries, specialising in Inuit and Northwest Coast sculpture, graphic art and jewellery.

206 Cambie St, Gastown.
Tel: (604) 688 7323; www.inuit.com

Khot-La-Cha

Authentic Coast Salish handicrafts on sale include carvings, moose-hide crafts, clothing and porcupine-quill jewellery.

270 Whonoak St, North Vancouver.
Tel: (604) 987 3339;
www.khot-la-cha.com

Trading Post

Native artists still come to this restored 1911 log cabin near the famous Capilano Suspension Bridge to sell their work. Items include spirit masks, jewellery, knitwear and leatherware.

3735 Capilano Rd, North Vancouver.
Tel: (604) 985 7474; www.capbridge.com.
Open: daily.

Shopping

Take home some traditional handmade gifts

Clothing

Angel

The clothing here is 'wearable art', with bright, hand-painted garments for children and adults by Jackie Haliburton.
2 Powell St. Tel: (604) 681 0947; www.angelpaint.com

Dream Apparel & Articles for People

Locally designed hip and comfortable urban wear in Gastown, with a Granville Island location.
311 West Cordova St. Tel: (604) 683 7326; Also **Little Dream**, *130-1666 Johnston St, Granville Island (tel: (604) 683 6930); http://dreamvancouver.com*

Edie Hats

Chapeaux galore on Granville Island are found in a fun shop that guarantees to turn around Vancouverites' rainy day bad hair.
4-1666 Johnston St, Granville Island. Tel: (604) 683 4280, freephone (800) 750 2134; http://ediehats.com

Leather Ranch

A huge selection of quality leather and suede fashions and accessories.
Suite 302, 1150 Douglas St, Victoria. Tel: (250) 384 4217; www.leather-ranch.com

OK Boot Corral

Western boots, hats, belts, buckles, bolo ties and souvenirs of the Old West.
205 Carrall St, Gastown. Tel: (604) 684 2668; www.okbootcorral.com

Repp Big and Tall

Casual and smart clothing for big, tall guys, with tailoring available on the premises for quick alterations.

475 West Hastings St. Tel: (604) 681 3548; www.mrbigandtall.ca

Roots Canada

Established in 1973, Roots now has more than 80 stores across the country, including 16 BC locations, selling its own line of rugged, casual clothing for the family.
1001 Robson St (tel: (604) 683 4305); Metrotown Centre, Burnaby (tel: (604) 435 5554); Suite 621, 3147 Douglas St (Mayfair), Victoria (tel: (250) 383 7221); and **Robson Kids**, *1153 Robson St (tel: (604) 684 8801); http://canada.roots.com*

Silk Weaving Studio

Fine-quality, hand-dyed and woven silk clothing, accessories and jewellery.
1531 Johnston St, Granville Island. Tel: (604) 687 7455; www.silkweavingstudio.com

Tall Girl

This store offers fashion, sportswear, footwear, lingerie and sleepwear, in a range of sizes all designed for tall, long-waisted or long-legged figures.
644 Hornby St. Tel: (604) 688 9238; www.tallgirlshop.com

Tilley Endurables

Travel and adventure clothing, including the famous Tilley hat – it floats, ties on, repels rain, won't shrink and comes with a lifetime guarantee and a four-page owner's manual!
2401 Granville St. Tel: (604) 732 4287; www.tilleyvancouver.com

True Value Vintage Clothing

You can buy, sell, trade and hire vintage clothing here, or you can just browse around the range of garments and accessories from the 1920s to the 1970s. *710 Robson St. Tel: (604) 685 5403.*

Woo Vintage

Specialising in vintage apparel from the 1950s, 1960s and 1970s, with the stated intention to 'woo' classic clothing fans, this shop moved to its new location in 2010.

4366 Main and 28th Sts.
Tel: (604) 687 8200;
www.woovintage.com

Gifts, souvenirs and specialist stores

The Boardroom

Meetings are not on the agenda here, but skateboards, snowboards, wakeboards and surfboards are. This multi-season gear shop has three Vancouver shops; one has clearance items at good prices.

1745 W 4th Ave (tel: (604) 734 7669);

2057 Lonsdale Ave, North Vancouver (tel: (604) 985 9669); and Boardroom Clearance, 1717 W 4th Ave (tel: (604) 742 0032); www.theboardroomshop.com

Chocolate Arts

Chocolate medallions with Haida designs.

2037 W 4th Ave. Tel: (604) 739 0475; www.chocolatearts.com. Open: Mon–Sat 10am–6pm, Sun noon–5pm.

Grand Maple

Quality Canadian souvenirs, including a large collection of BC jade and, of course, maple syrup.

1046 Robson St. Tel: (604) 681 8979.

Industrial Revolution

Sleek, modern home furnishings.

2306 Granville St. Tel: (604) 734 4395; www.industrialrevolution.net

Lululemon

Trendy yoga apparel with a designer West Coast twist, that started in Vancouver. Many locations also offer

Shoppers can browse well into the evening

Shopping

A street stall in Chinatown

yoga and pilates classes. Vancouver's **lululemon lab**, where new designs are sketched, also tries out and sells the lab-tested wear.

1148 Robson St (tel: (604) 681 3118); **Lab***: 511 W Broadway (tel: (604) 708 1126); www.lululemon.com*

Mountain Equipment Co-op (MEC)

Outdoor gear and clothing, much of it made in Canada, with a slight discount for members who buy an inexpensive lifetime membership. Look for trendy, up-to-date styles with lots of hands-on practical advice.

130 W Broadway (tel: (604) 872 7858); 1341 Main St, North Vancouver (tel: (604) 990 4417); and 1450 Government St, Victoria (tel: (250) 386 2667); www.mec.ca

New-Small and Sterling

Functional and decorative contemporary glass designs in the gallery and hot shop glass-blowing demonstrations.

1440 Old Bridge St, Granville Island. Tel: (604) 681 6730; www.hotstudioglass.com

The Umbrella Shop

Now into its third generation, this family business has an in-house factory making a large selection of umbrellas to complement imported ones.

1106 W Broadway. Tel: (604) 669 9444; www.theumbrellashop.com. Open for tours and shopping: Mon–Sat 10am–6pm.

Markets

Vancouver's markets are lively and entertaining places to shop. In a party atmosphere of street entertainment and fast food, you can browse around stalls selling Canadian crafts, souvenirs, designer kitchenware, flowers and all kinds of fresh produce.

Granville Island Public Market

The oldest of several waterfront markets, this farmer's market includes greengrocers, fishmongers, artisan bakeries, flowers and food to take away or have a picnic on a broad outdoor deck overlooking the marine activity in False Creek.

On Granville Island; accessible by AquaBus (tel: (604) 689 5858; www.theaquabus.com) from the foot of Granville St. www.granvilleisland.com

Lonsdale Quay Market

Highlights among the wide selections of goods available are The Forest Studio (*tel: (604) 990 8281*) for gems and stones, and Allyado (*tel: (604) 988 2200*) for luggage and travel goods.
123 Carrie Cates Court, North Vancouver; accessible by SeaBus (www.translink.ca) from downtown. Tel: (604) 985 6261; www.lonsdalequay.com

Park Royal Market

Visiting Park Royal is like doing a tour of Europe, with its Belgian bakery, German deli, Italian pasta outlets, Scottish butcher and international newsstand.
Park Royal South, Marine Dr, West Vancouver. Tel: (604) 922 3211; www.shopparkroyal.com

River Market at Westminster Quay

Getting here is half the fun, involving a spectacular 25-minute ride by SkyTrain from downtown. The market, renovated in 2010, overlooks the Fraser River.
810 Quayside. Tel: (604) 520 3881; www.rivermarket.ca

Robson Public Market

On the upstairs level, artisan-vendors and a cluster of cafés have the impressive backdrop of a 43m (141ft) long mural depicting life in the West End – all overlooking the colourful displays of produce below.
1610 Robson St. Tel: (604) 682 2733; www.robsonpublicmarket.com

Vancouver Flea Market

Over 360 stalls vie for business in the city's largest flea market, where you can bargain for unusual souvenirs.

Granville Island Public Market beside False Creek

703 Terminal Ave, five-minutes' walk from Main St. Tel: (604) 685 0666; www.vancouverfleamarket.com. Open: Sat & Sun 9am–5pm, holidays 9am–4pm.

Shopping malls

The Landing

This beautifully restored heritage building houses an exceptional range of elegant fashion stores and speciality goods, and a selection of fine restaurants.
375 Water St. Tel: (604) 483 5050; www.the-landing.com

Landsdowne Centre

Five minutes' drive from the airport, this mall has more than 130 shops, including department stores, designer fashion boutiques and many speciality shops.
5300 No 3 Rd and Alderbridge Way, Richmond. Tel: (604) 270 1344; http://landsdowne-centre.com

Metrotown Centre

Greater Vancouver's and BC's largest shopping complex, just 15 minutes from downtown, with over 450 stores. All the big names and plenty of independents are represented here, and there are special events to entertain shoppers. At Metropolis, start by dropping in at the customer service kiosk at the mall to ask for orientation. Metropolis includes the largest food court in western Canada, meaning you'll have plenty of variety to choose from when you've worked up an appetite shopping. Station Square has the Holiday Inn Express (*tel: (604) 438 1881*) and there are cinemas.
4800 Kingsway, Burnaby. Tel: (604) 438 4715; www.metropolismetrotown.com

Oakridge Centre

Over 150 quality stores here enjoy a bright and airy environment, with 20m

The glass rotunda at the Pacific Centre mall

Light and bright Oakridge Centre

(66ft) high vaulted skylights. There is also a cineplex.

60 W 41st Ave. Tel: (604) 261 2511; www.shopping.ca

Pacific Centre

This mall spreads over and under three downtown city blocks, where a three-storey waterfall, a glass rotunda and a skylit atrium attempt to bring the outdoors indoors. The redeveloped shopping centre features the Holt Renfrew Department Store and about 160 other stores.

701 W Georgia St. Tel: (604) 688 7235; www.pacificcentre.ca

Park Royal Mall

This mall opened more than 40 years ago, when it was Canada's first major shopping centre. It has over 200 stores, half of which are independent traders.

2002 Park Royal South, at the foot of the Lions Gate Bridge, West Vancouver. Tel: (604) 925 9576; www.shopparkroyal.com

Richmond Centre

All the usual department stores and international chains are gathered in this large mall, with a total of 240 stores, near the airport.

6551 No 3 Rd and Westminster Highway. Tel: (604) 713 7467; www.richmondcentre.com

Sinclair Centre

This restored historic building houses a small cluster of exclusive shops circling an elegant skylit atrium, where musicians entertain and artists display their works.

757 W Hastings St. Tel: (604) 488 0672; www.sinclaircentre.com

Entertainment

Few people come to Vancouver for entertainment, except for the outdoor variety so bountifully offered by Mother Nature. But Vancouver is a quietly vibrant city and does offer indoor options such as ballet, opera, classical music, rock, jazz, theatre and cinema, featuring respectable local, national and international talent.

The daily newspapers, *The Vancouver Sun* (*www.vancouversun.com*) and *The Province* (*www.theprovince.com*), along with the free weeklies, the *Westender* (*www.westender.com*) and *Georgia Straight* (*www.straight.com*), contain advertising and editorial reviews of current entertainment. *WHERE Vancouver* (*http://where.ca/vancouver*), a free, compact monthly magazine in most hotels, provides details of musical and theatrical performances, along with listings of cabarets, clubs and jazz gigs.

The **Coastal Jazz and Blues Society** (*tel: (604) 872 5200, (888) 438 5200; www.coastaljazz.ca*) offers information on the jazz scene. For recorded information on current films and cinema locations, call the cineplex for the local area or the individual independent cinemas; most have website information, including matinee and other discounts.

All kinds of street entertainers perform throughout the city, but especially on Robson Street. However, some of the best shows materialise on **Granville Island** on sunny Sunday afternoons. On the wooden deck in front of the market overlooking False Creek, jugglers, clowns, storytellers, mime artists and musicians vie for attention. More formal outdoor concerts are presented at the Dr Sun Yat-Sen Chinese Garden on Carrall Street in Chinatown, with Friday 'Enchanted Evenings Concerts' from early July to Labour Day Weekend (*tel: (604) 662 3207; www.vancouverchinesegarden.com*).

Tickets

Ticketmaster (*tel: (604) 280 4444; www.ticketmaster.ca*) sells tickets for cultural and sporting events. Locations in downtown Vancouver are convenient (*Tourism Vancouver, 200 Burrard St; General Motors Place, 800 Griffiths Way; and Van City Sports, 554 W Georgia St*). Ticketmaster has special lines for arts events (*tel: (604) 280 3311*) and spectator sports (*tel: (604) 280 4400*). For half-price day-of-show tickets, call **Tickets Tonight**, *tel: (604) 684 2787.*

Ballet, opera and classical music

Ballet BC (*tel: (604) 732 5003; www.balletbc.com*), **Canada's Royal Winnipeg Ballet** and such well-known visiting dance companies as the Kiev Ballet perform at the 2,800-seat Queen Elizabeth Theatre (*630 Hamilton St; http://vancouver.ca*).

Also at the Queen Elizabeth, the **Vancouver Opera** (*tel: (604) 682 2871; www.vancouveropera.ca*) and visiting opera companies present contemporary productions and such timeless masterpieces as *The Marriage of Figaro* and *Don Pasquale*. At the adjacent **Vancouver Playhouse Theatre Company** (*tel: (604) 873 3311; www.vancouverplayhouse.com*), the **Vancouver East Cultural Centre** (*tel: (604) 251 1363; www.thecultch.com*), or, as it's affectionately known to locals, 'The Cultch', has an impressive programme of avant-garde theatre, international music, festivals and other arts events.

Many musical events are also held at the gracious and elegant **Orpheum**, located at 884 Granville, Smithe and Seymour (*tel: (604) 665 3035*). The Orpheum is the home of the Vancouver Symphony Orchestra (*tel: (604) 665 3050; http://vancouver.bc.ca/commsvcs/cultural/theatres*), which also performs at other Lower Mainland venues and at several outdoor locations during the summer. It is also the home of the Bach Choir, Chamber Choir and Cantata Singers, and is the BC Entertainment Hall of Fame venue.

Several classical chamber music groups run by professional musicians present complimentary concerts at a number of public sites. Free lunchtime concerts are often held on the plaza in Robson Square and in shopping malls around the city during July and August. **Music in the Morning** (*tel: (604) 873 4612; www.musicinthemorning.org*) offers classical concerts for people on the go: Music in the Morning; Composers & Coffee; and Rush Hour, in venues such as the Vancouver Art Gallery and the Vancouver Academy of Music.

Headphones for people with hearing impairment are available at the Queen Elizabeth Theatre, the Vancouver Playhouse and the Orpheum. All these places are wheelchair-accessible. For more information on Vancouver theatres, *tel: (604) 665 3050*, or visit *http://vancouver.ca/theatres*

Open-air performances are always a big draw

Bard on the Beach

The **Bard on the Beach Shakespeare Festival** (*tel: (604) 739 0559, freephone (877) 739 0559; www.bardonthebeach. org*) presents Shakespearean favourites in an open-ended candy-striped tent seating 300 people in Vanier Park, adjacent to the Planetarium, on evenings from June to September. The setting is spectacular, as the stage has a backdrop of the North Shore Mountains and sky coloured by the setting sun. Prices are reasonable, and reservations are recommended.

Casinos

Gambling is highly regulated in Canada. Each province has its own laws and regulations. In BC, for those who are 19 or older, there are slot machines and table games in casinos. A large portion of the proceeds goes to local charities. The Great Canadian Gaming Corporation (*www.greatcanadiancasinos. com*) has nine locations in BC. The **Edgewater Casino** (*311-750 Pacific Boulevard South; tel: (604) 687 3343; www.edgewatercasino.ca*), in False Creek between BC Place and GM Place, is in downtown Vancouver. Horse racing, bingo and a provincial lottery are other options.

Cinema

Vancouver has dozens of cinemas showing the latest feature films. Most are to be found downtown on the Granville Street Mall. Metrotown Centre at Burnaby has SilverCity Metropolis (*tel: (604) 435 1999*); the **Pacific Cinémateque**, at 1131 Howe Street (*24-hour hotline: (604) 688 FILM; www.cinematheque.bc.ca*), is a non-profit, educational society dedicated to the enjoyment and study of film. Emphasis is on independent, non-mainstream films and classics.

Esplanade 6 Cinemas is at 200 West Esplanade, North Vancouver (*tel: (604) 983 2762; www.empiretheatres.com*). **Station Square 7 Cineplex** is at 220-6200 McKay Avenue, Burnaby (*tel: (604) 434 7711; www.cineplex.com*).

The Ridge, at 3131 Arbutus Street (*tel: (604) 738 6311; www. festivalcinemas.ca*), also features the classical and offbeat, with 'love seat' arrangements to lift up the seat arm for 'snuggling with a partner'. Film theatre giant Cineplex (*www.cineplex.com*) runs several film complexes in Vancouver and the surrounding neighbourhoods. There's **Station Square** at 220-2600 McKay Avenue, in Burnaby (*tel: (604) 434 7711*) and **Richmond Centre 6** at 6551 No 3 Road in the Richmond Shopping Centre (*tel: (604) 273 7173*). The **Scotiabank Theatre Vancouver** is downtown at 900 Burrard Street (*tel: (604) 630 1407*). The **Cineplex Odeon Park & Tilford** is in North Vancouver at 200-333 Brooksbank Avenue (*tel: (604) 985 4215*). **Cinemark Tinseltown** is also downtown at 88 West Pender (*tel: (604) 806 0799*).

For those seeking the biggest of the big screens, there are several IMAX/OMNIMAX locations: OMNIMAX®

Vancouver International Film Centre hosts the annual film festival

Theatre at Science World (*tel: (604) 443 7510; www.scienceworld.ca/omnimax*); **SilverCity Riverport IMAX®** (*14211 Entertainment Way, Richmond; tel: (604) 277 5993*); and **Colossus Langley** (*20090 No 91A Ave, Langley; tel: (604) 513 8747*); both *www. cineplex.com*

The annual **Vancouver International Film Festival** (*tel: (604) 685 8297; www.viff.org*), which takes place in September to October, offers the best in cinema from around the world.

Dinner plus

Blarney Stone

This lively Gastown restaurant features Irish and contemporary entertainment, starting at 7pm.
216 Carrall St. Tel: (604) 687 4322; http://blarneystone.ca

Shark Club Bar & Grill

This sports bar provides a warm ambience, created by a fireplace and rich mahogany surroundings. Sports fans enjoy the sports memorabilia, pool tables, dartboards and television broadcasts.

180 W Georgia St. Tel: (604) 687 4275; www.sharkclubs.com

Discos and clubs

AuBAR

Fast dancing, candles on the table and romance – go Thursday, Friday or Saturday.
674 Seymour St. Tel: (604) 648 2227; www.aubarnightclub.com

Bacchus

The bar/lounge in the Wedgewood Hotel is the place to go if you want to rub shoulders with celebs in town for Vancouver's hot film production scene.
845 Hornby St. Tel: (604) 608 5319; www.wedgewoodhotel.com

The Cellar Nightclub

Live house bands – BritRock and top-yo & hip hop, and comedy.
1006 Granville St. Tel: (604) 605 4350; www.cellarvan.com

Ginger Sixty-Two

A posh Fellini-esque ambience with a multitude of music styles.
1219 Granville St. Tel: (604) 678 8991; www.ginger62.com

Pop Opera

Sound pounds the walls and VIP areas of this be-seen lounge where Vancouver Canuck (hockey team) players have been spotted.

686 W Hastings St. Tel: (604) 633 3988; http://popopera.ca

Richards on Richards

Show up early to beat the lines, then stay to dance all night. Popular with the hip dance-floor crowd, the club has an upstairs bar and balcony for checking out the scene.

1036 Richards St.
Tel: (604) 687 6794;
www.richardsonrichards.com

Shine Nightclub

A trendy club that looks like *A Clockwork Orange*, all white and glossy.
364 Water St, Gastown.
Tel: (604) 408 4321;
http://shinenightclub.com

Vanilla Room

High above Langley in high style. Faux fur and leather décor, 'virtual art tables' and VIP service.
6001 No 196A St, Langley.
Tel: (604) 530 2026.

Venue

Rock, electric and one-night appearance events are the trendy club's forte.
881 Granville St. Tel: (604) 646 0064; www.venuelive.ca

The Yale

The Vancouver centre for live rhythm and blues music every day.
1300 Granville St. Tel: (604) 681 9253; www.theyale.ca

Jazz

There are many good jazz artists and good places to enjoy them in Vancouver (*http://vancouverjazz.com*). Evenings offer a good choice, including the **Backstage Lounge** at 1585 Johnston Street, Granville Island (*tel: (604) 687 1354; www.thebackstagelounge.com*). The **Cellar Restaurant Jazz Club**, on 3611 West Broadway (*tel: (604) 738 1959; www.cellarjazz.com*), features blues and cool jazz with name players and new talent. **Café Deux Soleils**, 2096 Commercial Drive (*tel: (604) 254 1195; www.cafedeuxsoleils.com*), is the home of live entertainment; the schedule changes frequently. The annual **Vancouver International Jazz Festival** is held throughout Vancouver in late June. For more information, call the **Jazz Hotline** (*tel: (604) 872 5200*) or visit *www.coastaljazz.ca*

Rock and contemporary music

Big Canadian and international names entertain regularly at **BC Place Stadium** (*tel: (604) 669 2300; www.bcplacestadium. com*), which seats 60,000 people, and in 2011 will reopen with an all-season retractable roof; **Thunderbird Arena** at 6081 Thunderbird Boulevard at the UBC campus (*tel: (604) 822 6121; www.thunderbirdarena.com*); the **Pacific Coliseum** (*tel: (604) 253 2311; www.pne.ca*) by the Pacific National Exhibition grounds; and **GM Place** (*800 Griffiths Way; tel: (604) 899 7400; www.generalmotorsplace.com*) – also known as The Garage, and home to

Vancouver's NHL Hockey Team, the Canucks.

Smaller places to hear good rock and local talent include **The Railway Club**, at 579 Dunsmuir (*tel: (604) 681 1625; www.therailwayclub.com*), and **Richards on Richards** at 1036 Richards Street (*tel: (604) 687 6794; www.richardsonrichards.com*). Check out *http://livevan.com* for up-to-date listings.

Theatre

The **Arts Club Theatre Company** (*tel: (604) 687 1644; www.artsclub.com*) offers the best in live theatre, ranging from classical Shakespeare to popular drama and contemporary works created by local playwrights. Programmes are presented year-round at the **Stanley Industrial Alliance Stage** (*2750 Granville St and 12th Ave*), **Granville Island Stage** (*next to the Granville Public Market*) and the **New Revue Stage** (*1601 Johnston St*). Also on Granville Island, the **Waterfront Theatre** (*1412 Cartwright St; tel: (604) 687 3005; www.giculturalsociety.org*) stages outstanding Canadian plays, while the adjacent **Carousel Theatre** (*tel: (604) 685 6217; www.carouseltheatre. ca*) entertains youngsters. The **Vancouver Playhouse Theatre Company** (*tel: (604) 873 3311; www.vancouverplayhouse.com*), housed in the same building as the **Queen Elizabeth Theatre** at 630 Hamilton Street downtown, stages six full-scale productions each season, including

classic and contemporary drama, comedy, musicals and at least one Canadian play. **Theatre Under the Stars** (*tel: (604) 734 1917; www.tuts.ca*) has been putting on Broadway-style musicals for half a century at the Malkin Bowl bandstand outdoors in Stanley Park. The show continues from mid-July to mid-August, weather permitting. It is especially fun to picnic under a full moon. The **Vancouver East Cultural Centre**, at 1895 Venables Street (*tel: (604) 251 1363; www.thecultch.com*), specialises in avant-garde theatre, complemented by visual art exhibitions.

The **TheatreSports League** presents hilarious improvisations, often involving the audience, at the Improv Centre, 1502 Duranleau Street, Granville Island (*tel: (604) 738 7013; www.vtsl.com*). At the **Lafflines Comedy Club**, 26 4th Street, New Westminster (*tel: (604) 525 2262; www.lafflines.com*), stand-up comics from all over the continent entertain from Thursday to Saturday.

The **Centre in Vancouver for Performing Arts**, at 777 Homer Street (*tel: (604) 602 0616; www.centreinvancouver.com*), features a variety of live performances, from musicals to solo performers, to ballet.

Every September, **Vancouver International Fringe Festival** (*tel: (604) 257 0350, infoline (604) 637 6830; www.vancouverfringe.com*) has many performances – from Shakespeare to avant-garde – in different venues.

Children

Vancouver offers an abundance of attractions to entertain and educate youngsters. Some activities mentioned here are described in more detail in other parts of this book. For more suggestions, check the easy-to-read and up-to-date www.findfamilyfun.com *and also* see p177.

Downtown

Aquarium

Kids enjoy touching the sea cucumbers, anemones, starfish and chitons (molluscs), and also love watching sea otters in a playful mood as they socialise underwater (*see pp66–7*). *Tel: (604) 659 3521; 24-hour info: (604) 659 3474; www.vanaqua.org*

For more water fun, there is the saltwater swimming pool – an enjoyable and safe option, which is supervised in summer by lifeguards at Second Beach; there are also the water parks on the sea wall near Lumberman's Arch and beside the fire engine playground near Pacific Avenue. Kids can cycle around the scenic 8.8km (5¹/₂-mile) Stanley Park section of the sea wall. Bicycle rentals are available near the Georgia Street entrance to the park.

H R MacMillan Space Centre

Take a virtual voyage through space, and learn about what it's like to live up in space. The Space Centre also has a planetarium.

1100 Chestnut St. Tel: (604) 738 7827; www.spacecentre.ca

Science World

Provides enough hands-on educational enjoyment for a whole day. The OMNIMAX® Theatre presents six shows daily (*see pp61–2*). *1455 Quebec St. Tel: (604) 443 7440; www.scienceworld.ca*

Stanley Park is a wonderful playground and children especially love the Miniature Train (*tel: (604) 257 8531; http://vancouver.ca*), the nearby Children's Farmyard animals, and the squirrels and raccoons which hang around Lost Lagoon. There are tours on horse-drawn wagons and carriage rides through the park (*tel: (604) 681 5115; www.stanleyparktours.com*) (*see pp63–4 and 66–7*).

Granville Island

Aquabus and SeaBus rides

The Aquabus (*www.theaquabus.com*) from Hornby Street to Granville Island is quick; visit such attractions as the

Kids Market. Or, take the SeaBus (*www.translink.ca*) to North Vancouver for spectacular views.

Arts Umbrella
Summer camp classes are run for kids up through to the age of 19. They include sculpture, dance and woodcarving. Reservations are advised. *1286 Cartwright St. Tel: (604) 681 5268; www.artsumbrella.com. Open: 9am–3.30pm (shorter for pre-school children).*

Families can share outdoor fun with lessons and rental kayaks from Ecomarine, at 1668 Duranleau Street (*tel: (604) 689 7575; www.ecomarine.com*).

Carousel Theatre
Fun shows for the younger set and their parents.
Waterfront Theatre, 1411 Cartwright St, Granville Island; tel: (604) 669 3410; www.carouseltheatre.ca

Kids Market
Houses two dozen shops and other diversions. Special events are organised for weekends. There is an Adventure Zone Toddler Zone for the very young. *1496 Cartwright St. Tel: (604) 689 8447; www.kidsmarket.ca. Open: daily 10am–6pm.*

Weary parents can revive themselves at Pedro's Organic Coffee House, while children shower each other with big fire hoses at the supervised Water Park in front.

East Vancouver and Burnaby
Burnaby's Heritage Village and Carousel (*tel: (604) 293 6501; www.burnabyvillagemuseum.ca*) is an open-air museum with carousel, costumed guides and old buildings re-creating life between the 1890s and 1920s.

Playland at the PNE (Pacific National Exhibition) Grounds
The rides are open from April to October. Attractions include the roller coaster, log-chute rides and the 'Breakdance' and 'Gladiator' rides. Watching chickens hatch and cows calve during the Pacific National Exhibition in the last two weeks of August is especially interesting. *Tel: (604) 253 2311; www.pne.ca*

North Vancouver
Capilano Suspension Bridge and Treetops – safe but scary, the suspension bridge hangs 70m (230ft) above a river and leads to a trail through unspoilt rainforest. Treetops Adventure offers a squirrel's-eye view. *Tel: (604) 985 7474; www.capbridge.com*
Maplewood Farm (*tel: (604) 929 5610; www.maplewoodfarm.bc.ca*) is a 2-hectare (5-acre) park where children can get acquainted with farm animals, have a pony ride and watch milking.

University of British Columbia
The **Museum of Anthropology** (*tel: (604) 822 5087; www.moa.ubc.ca*) lets children beat hanging drums and pull out dozens of drawers to examine First Nations toys, jewellery and clothing. Children enjoy feeding the fish at the Nitobe Memorial Garden (*www.nitobe.org*).

Sport and leisure

*Vancouver is an absolute mecca for sports-lovers. The long days of summer are great for golf and tennis; the beaches and sea breezes appeal to swimmers and sailors; there are lots of trails for cyclists and hikers; and local fresh and salt waters teem with life for eager anglers and divers. Come June, Vancouver hosts the Rio Tinto Alcan Dragon Boat Festival, North America's longest-running event of its kind (*http://dragonboat.ca*), and in winter skiers head for the mountains.*

Land sports

Bowling

Vancouver has many bowling alleys, some five-pin, some ten-pin. Check the Yellow Pages for details of opening times.

Bungee and ropes courses

Navigate the treetops, plunge head first off a bridge, or zipline through a canyon at **WildPlay**, an adventure park on Vancouver Island just outside Nanaimo. Kids aged 12 and over are welcome.
35 Nanaimo River Rd. Tel: (888) 716 7374; www.wildplay.com

Caving

There are about 2,000 caves in BC, mostly on Vancouver Island, all in original condition, with no walkways. Only 600 of them have been charted.

Popular caves for exploring include the Black Hole (situated in virgin rainforest), the Horne Lake Caves, Paradise Lost and the Artlish River Cave. Cody Caves offers one- and three-hour seasonal tours – including safety gear – at Cody Caves Provincial Park (*tel: (250) 505 2592; www.codycaves.ca*).

Cycling

The Stanley Park Seawall (*see pp68–9*) provides the perfect path for an hour of urban cycling. The paved trail following the SkyTrain route from Main Street station to New Westminster is also relatively flat and passes 32 parks and playgrounds. Spokes Bicycle Rentals (*tel: (604) 688 5141; www. vancouverbikerental.com*) and other downtown operations rent bicycles by the hour or by the day.

Golfing

Of the province's 200 golf courses, a number of them are in Vancouver, and all are open to the public. A letter of introduction from your home club provides entry to private courses. Several par-three courses are scattered throughout the city. Langara Golf

Course at 6706 Alberta Street (*tel: (604) 713 1816*) is one of the best in BC; another is the McCleery Golf Course in South Vancouver at 7188 MacDonald Street (*tel: (604) 257 8191*).

Hiking and walking

Most major parks in and around Vancouver have well-marked circuits for scenic wilderness hikes and walks. The Stanley Park Seawall is the best walk close to downtown (*see pp68–9*). Lynn Canyon is an equally spectacular, but a cheaper and quieter, alternative to Capilano (and it has its own suspension bridge). Lynn Canyon Ecology Centre on the North Shore (*tel: (604) 980 3755; www.dnv.org/ecology*) organises summer nature programmes about the environment.

Horse riding

Urban equestrians enjoy the trails at Langley 204 Equestrian Centre at 543 204th Street (*tel: (604) 533 7978*), which offers 18km (11 miles) of trails on good-quality horses. Riders with more time may want to rough it with wranglers on the range, such as the one at Ashcroft known as the Sundance Guest Ranch (*tel: (250) 453 2422, freephone (800) 553 3533; www.sundanceguestranch.com*).

Paragliding

Flightseeing is an exhilarating way to view the spectacular BC scenery for those who have the nerve. Mount Seven in the Rockies is a site of international competitions for paragliding and hang-gliding, but for a beginner's introduction to the sport flights in tandem with a professional pilot are available (weather permitting). Call Vancouver Island Paragliding (*tel: (250) 514 8595; www.viparagliding.com*).

Rock climbing

In a region with so many mountains, rock climbing is almost an instinct. Learners practise in Lighthouse Park in West Vancouver on cliffs overhanging the water, and then move on to tough mountain challenges. **Cliffhanger Indoor Rock Climbing Centre** (*tel: (604) 874 2400; www.cliffhangervancouver.com*) has nearly 1,000sq m (10,760sq ft) of walls to climb. **Playland** (*tel: (604) 253 2311*) offers an 11m (35ft) outdoor climbing wall in the Extreme Action Zone of the grounds. Contact the Federation of Mountain Clubs of BC (*tel: (604) 873 6096; www.mountainclubs.org*).

Skiing

Vancouver's North Shore has three ski areas within a half-hour drive of the city centre. The nearest is Grouse Mountain (*www.grousemountain.com*), where in good weather skiers enjoy spectacular views down to the city centre and across Georgia Strait.

Cypress Mountain (*http://cypressmountain.com*) to the west and Mount Seymour (*www.mountseymour.com*) to the east also offer Nordic

(*Cont. on p160*)

Taking to the slopes

BC is one of Canada's top snow sports playgrounds. The moderate climate and the proximity of Vancouver International Airport to good facilities, comfortable accommodation and challenging terrain appeal to people worldwide.

When moist, cold air from the Pacific meets the coastal mountains, the result is big flakes of snow which pack the mountain peaks and slopes.

The three North Shore Mountains, Cypress, Grouse and Seymour – all within a half-hour drive of Vancouver city centre – offer spectacular sea and city vistas, along with good ski facilities open day and evening from November to April when the snows permit.

Whistler/Blackcomb is one of the highest-rated ski areas in the world, and a featured 2010 Winter Olympic/Paralympic Games venue. A two-hour drive north from Vancouver, high-speed quad chairs and the PEAK 2 PEAK Gondola between Whistler and Blackcomb peaks transport skiers and snowboarders over spectacular slopes to a variety of runs for all levels, alpine chutes, moguls and vast areas of backcountry for skilled skiers.

Hemlock, in the Fraser Valley, also accommodates overnight guests at its cosy alpine village, and offers 13km (8 miles) of groomed cross-country trails. Manning Park Resort is a small, family-style ski area at the northern end of the Cascades.

Nordic skiing presents a range of exciting challenges. There are 16km (10 miles) of hilly tracks and packed trails at Hollyburn Ridge on Cypress Mountain. The Diamond Head area in Garibaldi Park has high glaciers, with an overnight hut available at Elfin Lakes. The Hemlock Valley loop comprises 29km (18 miles) of

SOME POPULAR SKI & SNOWBOARD RESORTS

Vancouver

Cypress Mountain. *Tel: (604) 419 7669; http://cypressmountain.com*
Grouse Mountain. *Tel: (604) 980 9311, (604) 986 6262; www. grousemountain.com*
Mount Seymour. *Tel: (604) 986 2261; www.mountseymour.com*

British Columbia

Big White Ski Resort, Kelowna. *Tel: (800) 663 2772; www.bigwhite.com*
Silver Star, Vernon. *Freephone: (800) 663 4431; www.skisilverstar.com*
Whistler/Blackcomb, Whistler. *Tel: (866) 218 9690; www.whistlerblackcomb.com*

groomed trails, good for both cross-country and Telemark skiing.

Other downhill and Nordic ski areas are scattered throughout the BC interior. Sun Peaks Resort (Okanagan, near Kamloops); and Fernie Alpine Resort, Kimberley Alpine Resort and Panorama Mountain Village (Kootenay Rockies); are known for gorgeous scenery to go with downhill skiing. For the adventurous, there is heli-skiing in the Bugaboos and at Tyax, north of Whistler, and there is snowcat skiing in the Selkirk Mountains.

BC is perfect for snow sports

skiing. Cypress and Grouse are lit for evening skiing until 10pm. All three mountains have equipment rentals and restaurants.

Tennis

Almost 200 public courts, scattered throughout the city, are free and operate on a first come, first served basis. Stanley Park requires reservations and charges a court fee in summer.

Watersports

Vancouver has water on three sides, and BC has vast coastline, thousands of islands, 11,000 rivers and creeks, 6,000 lakes, coastal marine parks and countless tidal inlets, offering unmatched opportunities for adventure (*see* Getting away from it all, *pp127–32*).

Canoeing

A number of companies specialise in outdoor adventures. They can arrange canoeing trips for half a day or week-long excursions with full catering. Lotus Land Tours (*tel: (604) 684 4922, freephone (800) 528 3531; www. lotuslandtours.com*) offers a half-day nature adventure with free pick-up in Vancouver.

Fishing

A licence (*www.discoverfishingbc.ca*) for salt water or fresh water or both, sold in major downtown department stores and in sporting goods shops as well as online, is required. The interior season extends from May to October, while coastal waters are year-round. Rivers and lakes contain trout and salmon. Arctic grayling, pike and walleye inhabit northern waters, while the boundary areas contain smallmouth bass and yellow perch. Sturgeon live in the Fraser and Columbia Rivers and bass are found on Vancouver Island.

Spring or chinook salmon and coho are the most popular saltwater catches, although some anglers prefer the challenges of sockeye, pink and chum salmon. Coastal waters also harbour halibut, flounder, sole, red snapper, perch, greenling, ling cod and the spotted sea-run cut-throat trout. Shellfish, abalones, clams, oysters, crabs, mussels, scallops, shrimps and prawns also inhabit these waters.

You can either take a fishing charter, which will look after everything, or rent a motorboat. Sooke Fishing Charters offers B&B and salmon fishing charter combination packages out of south Vancouver Island (*tel: (888) 430 7456; www.sookebnb.bc.ca*).

Watch expert boat racers skim over the waters

A killer whale at close quarters

Sewell's Marina (*tel: (604) 921 3474; www.sewellsmarina.com*) has both bareboat rentals and charter options.

Kayaking

Ecomarine at 1668 Duranleau Street (*tel: (604) 689 7575; www.ecomarine. com*), on Granville Island, rents kayaks all year round.

A two-hour rental allows ample time to glide along the quiet waters of False Creek past the market deck, the floating houseboat homes, Science World and the residential community along the south shore. Both one- and two-seater kayaks are available. Talaysay Tours has kayaking tours led by First Nations guides with a rich knowledge of local flora and fauna and native legends (*tel: (604) 628 8555, freephone (800) 605 4643; http://talaysay.com*).

Batstar Adventure Tours have well-organised, relaxed, fun kayaking tours along Vancouver Island, the BC coast, and into the wilderness of Pacific Rim National Park's Broken Islands Group using top-of-the-line equipment, luxury tents, with gourmet food (*freephone: (877) 449 1230; www.batstar.com*).

Motor boating

Canada's largest fleet of self-drive rental boats is moored in Horseshoe Bay, 17km (10$^1/_2$ miles) northwest of downtown. Here, Sewell's Marina (*tel: (604) 921 3474; www.sewellsmarina.com*) rents boats by the hour and longer – a great way to explore the coastline and nearby islands.

River rafting

In this exhilarating social sport, a dozen or so novices and a couple of expert guides challenge the white water. Such Vancouver companies as Hyak Wilderness Adventures (*freephone: (800) 663 7238; www.hyak.com*) offer trips varying from a heart-thumping afternoon ride to six-day trips through the stunning scenery along BC's most exciting rivers.

Scuba diving

BC's underwater world is a submarine jungle of graceful giant anemones, towering sea-whips, gorgonian corals and other marine life.

Howe Sound is one of the most popular diving areas, and at Porteau Cove, on its eastern shore, a Provincial Marine Park has been established, with sunken vessels forming an artificial reef.

Though the surface waters are reasonably warm, the temperature below the thermocline persists at about 10°C (50°F), so divers will need a 6mm (¼in) neoprene wetsuit or, even better, a custom drysuit.

Equipment is available for hire from a number of dive shops, including BC Dive and Kayak Adventures, at 1695 West 4th Avenue (*tel: (604) 732 1344, freephone (800) 960 0066; www.bcdive. com*). The International Diving Centre at 2572 Arbutus Street (*tel: (604) 736 2541, freephone (866) 432 3483; http:// diveidc.com*) organises day, weekend or longer trips.

Swimming

English Bay beaches offer good swimming in summer, but seekers of solitude may prefer Savary Island and Desolation Sound further north, where the waters are just as warm.

The freshwater pool at Second Beach in Stanley Park and Kitsilano (Kits) Pool (Vancouver's only saltwater pool) at 2305 Cornwall (*tel: (604) 731 0011*) are open from May to September.

Indoor pools at the University of British Columbia (UBC) Aquatics Centre at 6121 University Boulevard (*tel:*

Whale-watching is a popular excursion

(604) 822 4522; www.aquatics.ubc.ca), the Vancouver Aquatic Centre at 1050 Beach Avenue (*tel: (604) 665 3424*) and the downtown Vancouver YMCA at 955 Burrard Street (*tel: (604) 689 9622; www.vanymca.org*) are open day and evening throughout the year.

Check out *http://vancouver.ca* for a complete list of city beaches and pools.

Spectator sports
Horse racing

Horse racing takes place from mid-April to the end of November at Vancouver's Hastings Racecourse (*tel: (604) 254 1631, freephone (877) 977 7702; www.hastingspark.com*). Diners who place bets can watch the races on closed-circuit television, but the view of Mount Seymour across Burrard Inlet from the stands is so spectacular that it would be a shame to miss it.

Team sports

For those who enjoy the roar of the crowd, there are the Canadian Football League BC Lions (*tel: (604) 589 ROAR; www.bclions.com*), who play home games at BC Place Stadium (*777 Pacific Boulevard*); the Vancouver Canadians AAA minor league baseball team – one step below the major leagues – (*tel: (604) 872 5232; http://web. minorleaguebaseball.com*), who play at Nat Bailey Stadium (*4601 Ontario St at 30th Ave*); the Vancouver Whitecaps soccer team (*tel: (604) 669 9283; http://vancouvermls2011.com*), who play in BC Place Stadium); and, in

The Vancouver Canucks take on the Phoenix Coyotes

winter, the National Hockey League Vancouver Canucks (*tel: (604) 899 4610; http://canucks.nhl.com*) ice hockey team, who compete at General Motors Place downtown. Information on seasons, game times, venues and tickets is available from Tourism Vancouver (*tel: (604) 683 2000; www.tourismvancouver.com*).

Whale-watching

Watching these great mammals of the Pacific is a favourite spectator sport of both residents and visitors. Johnstone Strait, between Vancouver Island and the mainland, is home to the world's largest concentration of killer whales, normally seen from May to September.

These sheltered waters, about 400km (249 miles) northwest of Vancouver, are home to multiple pods, with approximately 80 killer whales (orcas) in a southern group and 200 in a northern

area. When conditions permit, you can listen with a hydrophone to orcas sounding their famous songs and clicks. The orcas have a low birth rate and a low mortality rate. The males may live for up to 50 years, while the females may live twice as long. Johnstone Strait is also home for many sea birds and bald eagles, salmon, seals, sea lions, porpoises, minke whales, humpback whales, harbour seals and Pacific white-sided dolphins.

Off the west coast of Vancouver Island, spring is the time to see the big grey whales migrating from Baja California to Alaska. Several companies, such as **Orca Spirit Adventures** (*freephone: (888) 672 6722; www.orcaspirit.com*), provide watching tours. Bring binoculars. **Vancouver Whale Watch** in Richmond guarantees sightings and uses zodiacs for water-level viewing (*tel: (604) 274 9565; www.vancouverwhalewatch.com*).

drink

...in Vancouver in an amazing variety of ... Asian, some European, some African, ...can, and others which artfully combine ...reate new cuisines. Chefs in Vancouver ...r Island take particular pride in using ...ients, whether fresh fish, locally raised ...or fruits, vegetables and herbs from the ...'Dining' with foods from a farmer's ...t any fresher.

Fine foods and wines are often cheaper in Vancouver than in Europe. Dinner usually costs more than lunch for the same menu, and breakfast is the bargain of the day. Many restaurants are closed on Monday. Except for fast-food places, reservations are recommended for lunch during the week and for dinner on Friday and Saturday evenings. Most restaurants accept credit cards. Restaurants do not add a service charge, so a tip of 15–20 per cent is welcome. Vegetarians will find plenty on menus, from salads to fresh vegetables.

Restaurants listed are categorised according to price per person for a full-course meal, not including alcohol.

★	under $10
★★	$10–25
★★★	$25–50
★★★★	over $50

Breakfast and brunch

Café Medina ★★
A European chef makes Belgian waffles and rich coffee.
556 Beatty St.
Tel: (604) 879 3114.

Elbow Room Café ★★
Plastered with photos of the rich and famous, this vibrates with energy.
560 Davie St.
Tel: (604) 685 3628.

James Street Café ★★
Big pancakes and a variety of eggs Benedict.
3819 Canada Way, Burnaby.
Tel: (604) 676 1876.

Sophie's Cosmic Café ★★
A great place to take kids for breakfast or for a snack at any time.
2095 W 4th Ave.
Tel: (604) 732 6810.

Sunshine Diner ★★
Top-notch food (especially breakfast, eggs and waffles), fast service.
2756 W Broadway.
Tel: (604) 733 7717.

Joe's Grill ★★★
Highly recommended for its delicious breakfasts and brunch.
2061 W 4th Ave in Kitsilano.
Tel: (604) 736 6588.

Chinese restaurants

Shao Lin Noodle Restaurant ★
Inexpensive but yummy noodle dishes in a busy atmosphere.

548 W Broadway.
Tel: (604) 873 1816.
**Hon's Wun-Tun
House ★★**
A popular place for
Cantonese cuisine.
1339 Robson St.
Tel: (604) 685 0871.
**Shanghai Xin Hua
Lou ★★**
Best dumplings in town
and dim sum.
4136 Main St.
Tel: (604) 879 5818.
Sun Sui Wah ★★
Good dim sum and
congee, and very popular.
3888 Main St.
Tel: (604) 872 8822.
**Szechuan Chongqing
Seafood Restaurant ★★**
Spicy Szechuan-style
food, lunch specials.
1668 W Broadway.
Tel: (604) 734 1668.
**Floata Seafood
Restaurant ★★★**
The biggest Chinese
banquet restaurant in the
heart of Chinatown.
400–180 Keefer St.
Tel: (604) 602 0368.

**Indian restaurants
Heaven and Earth India
Curry House ★★**
Authentic Indian cuisine,
sitar music and a relaxed
atmosphere.

1754 W 4th Ave.
Tel: (604) 732 5313.
Tandoori King ★★
A favourite among the
city's food specialists.
8017 Fraser St.
Tel: (604) 327 3355.
Vij's ★★★★
Wine-marinated lamb
popsicles get raves on a
lengthy mains menu.
1480 W 11th Ave.
Tel: (604) 736 6664.

**Japanese restaurants
Hapa Izakaya ★★**
You'll spot this popular
noodle place by the
queue forming outside
the door.
1479 Robson St.
Tel: (604) 689 4272.
Sui Sha Ya ★★
Fusion Japanese and all-
you-can-eat sushi.
101-1401 W Broadway.
Tel: (604) 733 8886.

Tanpopo ★★
One of Vancouver's first
all-you-can-eat sushi
spots and still serving
great sashimi. Frenzied
atmosphere but sushi
fanatics love it.
1122 Denman St.
Tel: (604) 681 7777.
Tojo's Restaurant ★★★★
One of the best in Canada.
1133 W Broadway.
Tel: (604) 872 8050.

**Other ethnic
restaurants
Dulcinea Chocolate
Café ★**
Many kinds of
chocolate libations
draw patrons to this
Spanish café.
1118 Denman St.
Tel: (604) 689 2699.
Hawkers Delight Deli ★
Singaporean Malay street
food, cash only.

A crêpe shop in laid-back Kitsilano

Enjoy fine cuisine in Cowichan Bay, Vancouver Island

4127 Main St.
Tel: (604) 709 8188.
East is East ★★
Small bowls meant to
share, superb chai, a
menu spanning India,
Turkey and Tibet, and
North African décor, near
UBC. Have the 'feast'.
3243 W Broadway.
Tel: (604) 734 5881.
**Afghan Horseman
Restaurant** ★★★
One room has floor
pillow seating. Huge
portions of Afghani
cuisine, occasional belly
dancers, and a potent
drink, the 'Mighty
Horseman'.
202-1833 Anderson St.
Tel: (604) 873 5923.
Nuba ★★★
Lebanese cuisine, with
lowered lights for
dinner, to evoke 1940s
Beirut.

207B W Hastings St.
Tel: (604) 688 1655.
Sanafir ★★★★
Three-way ingredient
tapas, with influences
from India and Southeast
Asia, Moroccan décor.
1026 Granville St.
Tel: (604) 678 1049.

Thai restaurant
**Montri's Thai
Restaurant** ★
City restaurateurs like to
dine here.
3629 W Broadway.
Tel: (604) 738 9888.

European restaurants
Omitsky Kosher Foods ★
Great Jewish deli food.
5866 Cambie St.
Tel: (604) 321 1818.
Athene's ★★
Family-run Greek,
generous portions, lively
environment.

3618 W Broadway.
Tel: (604) 731 4135.
**CinCin Ristorante
& Bar** ★★★
Contemporary Italian,
wood-fired grill,
stunning desserts.
1154 Robson St.
Tel: (604) 688 7338.
Lumière ★★★
French cuisine can be
enjoyed inside or on the
patio in fine weather.
Valet parking is a bonus.
2551 W Broadway.
Tel: (604) 739 8185.
**Lupo Restaurant
& Vinoteca** ★★★
Timeless Italian cuisine
in a Mediterranean-style
setting.
869 Hamilton St.
Tel: (604) 569 2535.
**The Chef and the
Carpenter** ★★★★
A top chef creates fine
French food here.
1745 Robson St.
Tel: (604) 687 2700.
Le Gavroche ★★★★
In the cosy and
charming upstairs of an
old house (the two
window tables offer a
great harbour view), Le
Gavroche has received
several awards for fine
cuisine, which ranges
from classic European

dishes to mahimahi and smoked duck.
1616 Alberni St.
Tel: (604) 685 3924.

Fast food
A&W ★
A favourite with younger children.
Sinclair Centre.
Tel: (604) 687 4186.

Babylon Café ★
Delicious chicken shawarma, takeaway only.
716 Robson St.
Tel: (604) 677 3522.

Café Crêpe ★
Sweet or savoury crêpes, made to order.
874 Granville St.
Tel: (604) 806 0845.

C-Lover's Fish & Chips ★
Tempura-like batter and great chips.
1660 Pemberton Ave.
Tel: (604) 980 9993.

Fogg n' Suds Restaurant ★
Fun and casual, with an international menu.
1323 Robson St.
Tel: (604) 683 2337.

Food Fair ★
There is fast food from many countries in this mall food area.
Pacific Centre, Howe & Dunsmuir Sts.

La Taquería ★
Modelled after a traditional Mexican taco stand, with tacos and quesadillas.
322 W Hastings St.
Tel: (604) 568 4406.

Vera's Burger Shack ★
Award-winning burgers.
1030 Davie St.
Tel: (604) 893 8372.

The Cactus Club ★★
Famous for Mexican fajitas and burgers.
1136 Robson St.
Tel: (604) 687 3278.

Coco Noodle Express ★★
Among the best of the Japanese sushi and noodle houses.
382 Robson St.
Tel: (604) 609 2688.

Flying Wedge Pizza ★★
You pay a bit more, but great pizza. Numerous outlets in the city, but this one is in Vancouver's beautiful library.
207–345 Robson St.
Tel: (604) 689 7078.

Japa Dog ★★
Japanese toppings and condiments on hot dogs, cash only.
Stands: Burrard & Smithe Sts; Burrard & Pender Sts; Waterfront Station.

The Old Spaghetti Factory ★★
Good family fare – a great place to take children.
53 Water St, Gastown.
Tel: (604) 684 1288.

Fish restaurants
Go Fish! ★★
Fresh local seafood on Fisherman's Wharf.
1505 W 1st Ave.
Tel: (604) 730 5039.

Bridges Restaurant ★★★
Eat your fish on the outdoor patio near the Granville Island Public Market.
1696 Duranleau St.
Tel: (604) 687 4400.

C ★★★
Dubbed downtown Vancouver's most innovative and creative seafood restaurant – try the octopus-wrapped scallops or soft-shell crab.
2-1600 Howe St.
Tel: (604) 681 1164.

COAST ★★★★
Try the oyster and chowder bar, then explore sushi, fish and chips and every seafood in between.
1054 Alberni St.
Tel: (604) 685 5010.

The Fish House in Stanley Park ★★★★

Exceptional seafood and fresh oyster bar, with sunny patios overlooking English Bay.
8901 Stanley Park Dr.
Tel: (604) 681 7275.

Places to talk

La Bodega Restaurant & Tapas Bar ★★

Tasty tapas here include the best fried chicken in town, and a lovely informal atmosphere.
1277 Howe St.
Tel: (604) 684 8814.

Fairmont Hotel Vancouver Lounge ★★

One of the city's great meeting places.
900 W Georgia St.
Tel: (604) 684 3131.

Indica Restaurant ★★

Indian-inspired cuisine in an intimate environment.
1795 Pendrell St.
Tel: (604) 609 3530.

Sylvia Hotel Bar ★★

Watch the sun set over English Bay.
Beach Ave & Gilford St.
Tel: (604) 681 9321.

Joe Fortes Seafood & Chop House ★★★

Haunt of yuppies, and a good place for people-watching.

777 Thurlow St.
Tel: (604) 669 1940.

Pan Pacific Lobby Lounge ★★★

Spectacular views of the Alaska cruise ships and the harbour.
999 Canada Place.
Tel: (604) 662 8111.

Seawall Bar and Grill ★★★

A cosy place in West Coast nautical style that is comfortable even when packed.
Bayshore Hotel, 1601 W Bayshore Dr.
Tel: (604) 691 6967.

Bacchus Restaurant & Lounge ★★★★

The place in town for mood lighting, quiet conversation and a good chance of spotting well-known celebrities.
845 Hornby St.
Tel: (604) 689 7777.

Seasons in the Park ★★★★

A view of Vancouver from Queen Elizabeth Park. Try weekend brunch.
Cambie St & W 33rd Ave.
Tel: (604) 874 8008.

Top of Vancouver Revolving Restaurant ★★★★

All of Vancouver in an hour above the Harbour Centre's Vancouver Lookout.
555 W Hastings St.
Tel: (604) 669 2220.

Vegetarian food

Dharma Kitchen ★

Completely vegan – no animal products of any kind. Specialises in rice bowls, Point Grey area.
3667 W Broadway.
Tel: (604) 738 3899.

Planet Veg ★

Fast vegetarian near Kitsilano Beach; indoor and outdoor seating.
1941 Cornwall Ave.
Tel: (604) 734 1001.

Greens & Gourmet Natural Foods Restaurant ★★

Soft new-age music, bright greenery-filled rooms and fine vegetarian cuisine, in Kitsilano.
2582 W Broadway.
Tel: (604) 737 7373.

The Naam ★★

A famous 24-hour vegetarian restaurant in Kitsilano, with a wood fireplace and heated patio.
2724 W 4th Ave.
Tel: (604) 738 7151.

Rime ★★

Tasty vegetarian entrées at this Turkish

Food and drink

The Pan Pacific has great harbour views

restaurant, in the Grandview-Woodlands district. Live entertainment.
1130 Commercial Dr.
Tel: (604) 215 1130.

Bodhi Choi Heung Vegetarian Restaurant ★★★
Provides good, meat-free meals.
3932 Fraser St.
Tel: (604) 873 3848.

West Coast

Café Madeleine ★★
No madeleines on the menu, but the sandwiches are excellent; a favourite with University of British Columbia students.
3763 W 10th Ave.
Tel: (604) 224 5558.

Memphis Blues Barbeque House ★★
Southern US barbecue is not Canadian, but the generous meat portions with all the fixin's (side dishes) are.
1465 W Broadway.
Tel: (604) 738 6806.

The Only Seafood Café ★★
The 'only' theme is carried on beyond its name – it only serves fish, only perfect, and is the only restaurant in town without a toilet!
20 E Hastings St.
Tel: (604) 681 6546.

Delilah's ★★★
The old railroad-style menus here offer a set-price, two-course and five-course dinner.

1789 Comox St.
Tel: (604) 687 3424

The Salmon House on the Hill ★★★
Salmon is barbecued over alderwood here, and the view over the city from this West Vancouver spot is spectacular.
2229 Folkstone Way.
Tel: (604) 926 3212.

Salt Tasting Room ★★★
Select local meat, cheese and wine.
45 Blood Alley, Gastown.
Tel: (604) 633 1912.

Transcontinental Restaurant ★★★
Classic surf and turf in the gorgeously remodelled CPR terminus.
601 West Cordova St.
Tel: (604) 678 8000.

Bishop's ★★★★
Consistently praised for its impeccable service, Bishop's also has an extensive cellar of Californian and Pacific Northwest wines.
2183 W 4th Ave.
Tel: (604) 738 2025.

Boneta Restaurant ★★★★
Pork belly, prime rib, lamb loin, halibut and traditional starters are dinnertime comfort food.
1 Cordova St West.
Tel: (604) 684 1844.

The Observatory at Grouse Mountain ★★★★

The magnificent views from the summit, and the inclusive Skyride trip up the mountain, are just two good reasons to dine at the Observatory. The superbly cooked West Coast specialities would be worth doing the 'Grouse Grind' hike for.

6400 Nancy Greene Way, Grouse Mountain, North Vancouver.
Tel: (604) 980 9311.

Raincity Grill ★★★★

A restaurant with a sound 'buy local, eat seasonal' ethic. This is a gem and it always makes 'best' lists.

1193 Denman St.
Tel: (604) 685 7337.

West ★★★★

Named the best restaurant in Vancouver, West takes French food and gives it a mouthwatering West Coast twist!

2881 Granville St.
Tel: (604) 738 8938.

Victoria

FooAsian Street Food ★

Asian street vendor cuisine, and signature Vietnamese ginger caramel chicken.

769 Yates St.
Tel: (250) 383 3111.

Sam's Deli ★

Popular soup and sandwich lunch spot across the street from the harbour.

805 Government St.
Tel: (250) 382 8424.

J+J Wonton Noodle House ★★

A local favourite, the best noodles and fresh seafood.

1012 Fort St.
Tel: (250) 383 0680.

Millos ★★

Look for a blue and white windmill downtown for great Greek food and entertainment.

716 Burdett Ave.
Tel: (250) 382 4422.

Bengal Lounge ★★★★

The Fairmont Empress' curry buffet and martinis. Very Raj.

721 Government St.
Tel: (250) 389 2727.

Camille's ★★★★

Good seasonal local food in the perfect spot for a romantic dinner.

45 Bastion Square.
Tel: (250) 381 3433.

Sooke Harbour House ★★★★

Spectacular views and a commitment to local ingredients.

1528 Whiffen Spit Rd, Sooke.
Tel: (250) 642 3421,
freephone (800) 889 9688.

Il Terrazzo ★★★★

About as good as northern Italian cuisine comes, with meals alfresco all year round by outdoor fireplaces if you choose.

555 Johnson St.
Tel: (250) 361 0028.

Pubs

There are few traditional British-style pubs in BC, probably because the province is too young, the population too transitory and the drinking laws too strict. Until the BC government first permitted neighbourhood pubs in the late 1960s, most public drinking was confined to hotels and restaurants. The pubs that do exist today include some good ones attached to local breweries. Good local brews, usually on tap, come from Steamworks Brewing, Yaletown Brewing Company, Granville Island Brewing and Whistler Brewing. There was also Horseshoe Bay Brewing, which, when it opened in 1981, was the first cottage brewery built in Canada in 50 years. It closed down in 2000.

Generally speaking, the further the watering hole from the big city, the friendlier the staff and the clientele.

Fanny Bay Inn ★★

This is one of the oldest pubs, built in 1938, and famous for its oysters, barbecued beef, pork and lamb, and staff who make visitors feel like locals.

4480 S Island Rd, near Courtenay, Vancouver Island.
Tel: (250) 335 2323.

Granville Island Brewing ★★

A fine selection of brews in one of Vancouver's favourite relaxation venues.

1441 Cartwright St.
Tel: (604) 687 2739.

Kingston Taphouse & Grille ★★

Contemporary urban pub and restaurant with six unique rooms in the heart of Vancouver.

755 Richards St.
Tel: (604) 681 7011.

The Lennox Pub ★★

Celtic touches, an outdoor patio, extensive beer and single malt scotch offerings.

800 Granville St.
Tel: (604) 408 0881.

Moose's Down Under Restaurant ★★

This Australian-style pub is open for breakfast, lunch and dinner.

830 W Pender St.
Tel: (604) 683 3300.

Spinnakers Gastro Brewpub ★★

Great beers accompany average food in this informal pub.

308 Catherine St,

Victoria West.
Tel: (250) 386 2739.

Steamworks Brewing Company ★★

A lovely old heritage building is the location of this pub, with good beer and home-made food.

375 Water St, Gastown.
Tel: (604) 689 2739.

Yaletown Brewing Company ★★

Right in the heart of trendy Yaletown. Pizzas are made in a traditional wood oven.

1111 Mainland St.
Tel: (604) 681 2739.

A tasting after the tour at Granville Island Brewing

Accommodation

BC accommodation ranges from rustic campsites to sybaritic suites with all amenities. Reservations are recommended, especially during the crowded days of summer and all holidays. The Tourism British Columbia Visitor Centre, at 200 Burrard Street, operates an accommodation reservation service where you may search for and book lodging through the website: www.hellobc.com. *You may also find special offers online.*

From Vancouver's high-rise and boutique hotels to country ranches and coastal cottages, British Columbia has a superb variety of places to stay for one night or much longer. One strategy can be to decide what kind of holiday – active adventure, luxury spa, out-in-nature, straightforward sightseeing, or museum and live performance cultural immersion – and seek the destination that best fits your dream. Then look at the range of accommodation available in a location convenient to your activities that is within your budget.

You may decide that it's worth it to splurge for a golf or spa resort or a once-in-a-lifetime flightseeing offered by the place where you're staying. Most luxury hotels have pools, a spa, a health club or fitness centre, restaurants, 24-hour room service and valet parking. Most are also wheelchair-accessible. Moderately priced hotels, from about $140–200 for a double room, are clean and comfortable, with some amenities.

Or, you may wish to economise, perhaps forgoing an en suite bath, and spend more on admissions or dining. There are also best-value, low-cost options below $75.

You can try something new, yurt camping in a provincial park or the rustic luxury of a remote fishing lodge.

Check if parking, local phone calls, international phone connections, Wi-Fi, fitness centre use, breakfast or other amenities are included in the room rate for free.

No book could cover all accommodations or be completely current. A short list of possible accommodations for you to consider follows; at a minimum, you will see a sampling of BC lodging, with rates, according to these categories:

★	under $75
★★	$75–140
★★★	$140–200
★★★★	over $200

Bed and breakfast

Greater Vancouver has numerous bed-and-breakfast establishments. When booking, enquire whether smoking is permitted, credit cards are accepted, and about special amenities, such as afternoon tea or wine sampling. To find a B&B, check British Columbia Bed & Breakfast Innkeepers Guild (*www.bcbestbnbs.com*).

Campsites

Several campsites are scattered throughout the city, but the Capilano RV Park (*tel: (604) 987 4722; www.capilanorvpark.com*) in North Vancouver has the most dramatic setting. There are sites for 190 motorhomes and 10 tents. The park has 24-hour-a-day supervision, a TV lounge, a whirlpool and a swimming pool. For BC provincial parks camping, reserve through *www.discovercamping.ca*

Best value

The Kingston Hotel Bed & Breakfast ★
Downtown. A complementary breakfast and discounts for senior citizens and students.
757 Richards St. www. kingstonhotelvancouver. com

Pillow Suites ★
Mount Pleasant. Homey and neat suites with fully equipped kitchens.
2875 Manitoba St. www.pillow.net

Shaughnessy Village ★
South Granville. Bed-and-breakfast guesthouse style, with views of Vancouver, free health club, gardens and adult toy yacht races.
1125 W 12th Ave. www.shaughnessyvillage. com

Simon Fraser University ★
Fairview Slopes. On the slopes of Burnaby Mountain, SFU offers spectacular views of the North Shore Mountains, the Pacific Ocean and Vancouver's lights.
8888 University Dr. www.sfu.ca/conference-accommodation

University of British Columbia ★
Point Grey. Single rooms with shared bath, studios, and one-bedroom suites.
5961 Student Union Boulevard. www.ubcconferences.com

Vancouver Youth Hostel ★
West End. Heaps of amenities and just minutes from shops, restaurants and beaches.
1114 Burnaby St. http://hihostels.ca

Cost-cutters

Barclay Hotel ★★
Downtown. A small European-style heritage hotel in the midst of Robson Street.
1348 Robson St. www.barclayhotel.com

Blue Horizon Hotel ★★
Downtown/West End. Best views are above floor ten for a romantic getaway with value rates.
1225 Robson St. www. bluehorizonhotel.com

Coast Coal Harbour Hotel ★★
Downtown. Minimalist design and a quiet location.
1180 W Hastings St. www.coasthotels.com

The Meridian At 910 Beach ★★
Downtown. Converted, kid-friendly, affordable condominium rooms

with plenty of space.
910 Beach Ave.
www.910beach.com

Moda Hotel ★★

Downtown. Small, cute and charming, especially suited for couples.
900 Seymour St.
www.modahotel.ca

Quality Hotel Downtown Vancouver ★★

Downtown. Better than basic accommodations for an excellent rate.
1335 Howe St.
www.choicehotels.ca

Riviera Hotel ★★

Downtown. One bedroom and family suites all with Robson Street or harbour views.
1431 Robson St.
http://rivieraonrobson.com

Rosedale on Robson Suite Hotel ★★

Downtown. A good, quiet, night's sleep in a safe, convenient location.
838 Hamilton St. www. rosedaleonrobson.com

Sylvia Hotel ★★

West End. A waterfront boutique hotel steps away from Stanley Park.
1154 Gilford St.
www.sylviahotel.com

The Victorian Hotel ★★–★★★

An 1898 downtown boutique hotel with a choice of en suite or hall bath.
514 Homer St.
www.victorianhotel.ca

Moderate upscale hotels

Best Western Chateau Granville ★★★

Suites close to downtown and Yaletown attractions.
1100 Granville St.
www.chateaugranville.com

Cascadia Hotel & Suites ★★★

Studio suites within easy walking distance of downtown, beaches, shopping and theatre.
1234 Hornby St. www. cascadiahotelvancouver. com

Delta Vancouver Suites Hotel ★★★

Downtown. A friendly, youthful feeling in an almost luxury-level-suite hotel.
550 W Hastings St. http:// delta-vancouver-suites. com

The Georgian Court Hotel ★★★

Comfortable hotel in trendy Yaletown with

free Wi-Fi, bicycles and umbrellas.
773 Beatty St.
www.georgiancourt.com

Hotel Le Soleil ★★★

Downtown. Discreet entrance on to a warm gold and red décor interior with warm, friendly staff.
567 Hornby St.
www.hotellesoleil.com

Intrawest Hotel ★★★

Downtown. All the mod cons plus telescopes in every room to see nature in Stanley Park or False Creek water activity.
Sheraton Wall Centre, 1088 Burrard St.
www.clubintrawest.com

Loden Hotel ★★★

Downtown. Manicured luxury, boutique amenities and attention, with no attitude to tarnish the hip elegance and flair.
1177 Melville St.
www.theloden.com

Opus Hotel Vancouver ★★★

Yaletown. Services and amenities of a small luxury hotel in a lifestyle-oriented environment.
322 Davie St.
www.opushotel.com

Pinnacle Hotel at the Pier ★★★

North Vancouver. A small hotel rising from a former shipyard and restored pier beside Lonsdale Quay, with spectacular city and mountain views.
138 Victory Ship Way.
www.
pinnaclehotelatthepier.com

Rosellen Suites at Stanley Park ★★★

West End. Large suites with fully equipped kitchens near the park.
2030 Barclay St.
www.rosellensuites.com

Sunset Inn & Suites ★★★

West End. Posh and a good getaway, suites with a full kitchen.
1111 Burnaby St.
www.sunsetinn.com

De luxe hotels

The Fairmont Hotel Vancouver ★★★★

Downtown. A city landmark for decades.
900 W Georgia St.
www.fairmont.com/
hotelvancouver

The Fairmont Waterfront ★★★★

Downtown. The elegant Waterfront sits across the street from Vancouver Harbour with stunning views of Stanley Park, downtown and North Vancouver.
900 Canada Place Way.
www.fairmont.com/
waterfront

Four Seasons Hotel Vancouver ★★★★

Downtown. The Four Seasons rises above more than 100 shops in Pacific Centre.
791 W Georgia St. www.
fourseasons.com/vancouver

L'Hermitage Hotel ★★★★

Downtown. Classy, fully appointed boutique hotel in a quiet downtown corner.
788 Richards St. www.
lhermitagevancouver.com

Pan Pacific Vancouver ★★★★

Downtown. Perches atop Canada Place with splendid views of Vancouver Harbour.
Suite 300, 999 Canada Place. www.panpacific.
com/Vancouver

Renaissance Vancouver Harbourside Hotel ★★★★

Downtown. Near Robson Street shopping and an easy trip to Stanley Park.
1133 West Hastings St.
www.renaissancevancouver.
com

Shangri-La Hotel Vancouver ★★★★

Downtown. Spacious, contemporary Asian-styled rooms, great service in Vancouver's landmark high-rise.
1166 Alberni St.
www.shangri-la.com

The Sutton Place Hotel ★★★★

Downtown. The luxury Sutton Place also manages the spacious flats in La Grande Résidence next door – minimum stay one month.
845 Burrard St. www.
vancouver.suttonplace.com

Wedgewood Hotel & Spa ★★★★

Downtown. Just a half-block from busy Robson Street, this European-style boutique hotel offers respite.
845 Hornby St.
www.wedgewoodhotel.com

Westin Bayshore and Marina ★★★★

Downtown. A rare downtown hotel with its own marina and yacht charter.
1601 Bayshore Dr.
www.westinbayshore.com

Practical guide

Arriving

Entry formalities

Citizenship and Immigration Canada is charged with providing information and enforcing regulations for visits to Canada. Check its 'Visiting Canada' website, *www.cic.gc.ca*, frequently, and near your travel dates, as requirements change. Requirements for all visitors include a valid full passport and a return or onward ticket, together with evidence of sufficient funds for the duration of your stay. Visas are not required for citizens of Britain, the Republic of Ireland, Australia, New Zealand and the USA. Visitors under 18 years of age unaccompanied by an adult must carry a letter from a parent or guardian granting permission to travel in Canada.

Visitors are only allowed to work in Canada if authorisation was obtained prior to entry into the country.

Numerous international airlines serve Vancouver with regularly scheduled flights from Europe, Asia, the South Pacific, the USA, Mexico and South America. Vancouver International Airport and Canada Customs and Immigration can be very busy in summer and at Christmas and Easter.

Customs and immigration (*www.cic.gc.ca*) regulations are strict, and baggage may be searched. Fruit and animal products may not be imported. There is no inbound duty-free shop.

Vancouver International Airport (YVR) is a 30-minute drive from downtown. Since it opened in 2009, the 25-minute SkyTrain Canada Line ride from YVR to downtown provides streamlined transportation. Taxis from Level 2 (Domestic Arrivals) cost $28–32 to go downtown. Aerocar (*freephone: (888) 821 0021*) provides limo service to downtown for $39. Passengers en route to Squamish and Whistler can take the YVR Whistler SkyLynx bus (*freephone: (800) 661 1725; www.pacificcoach.com*), and there is also a direct bus service to Victoria.

Camping

Camping is a wonderful way to enjoy fresh air and natural beauty and to make new friends, especially in summer. There are hundreds of campsites in BC, several of them in Greater Vancouver. The Capilano RV Park (*tel: (604) 987 4722; www.capilanorvpark.com*), a ten-minute drive across Lions Gate Bridge from the city centre, is one of the best urban camping areas in the world. Suburban campsites include Burnaby Cariboo RV Park (*tel: (604) 420 1722; www.bcrvpark.com*). Peace Arch RV Park (*tel: (604) 594 7009; www.peacearchrvpark.ca*) and Plaza RV Park (*tel: (604) 594 4440; www.plazarvpark.ca*) are in Surrey. The campsite at Porteau Cove Provincial Park (reservations: *www.discovercamping.ca*) overlooks Howe Sound, the most southerly fjord in North America. For an extensive listing of BC campsites, visit *www.env.gov.bc.ca*

Mountain Equipment Co-op (*130 W Broadway; tel: (604) 872 7858; www.mec.ca*) hires tents, camping equipment and other sporting goods.

For more information, check Tourism British Columbia's information online at *www.campingrvbc.com*

Children

Vancouver is a great place for a family holiday (*see pp154–5*). Children love the spacious parks and playgrounds to romp and roam. Public transport, whether on planes, trains, buses or ferries, offers reduced fares for youngsters, who particularly enjoy roaming around the decks of the big BC ferries. Most Vancouver attractions offer reduced admission prices for children.

Many hotels make an extra effort to cater to children, with special menus, reduced room rates and other services. The Westin Grand (*tel: (604) 602 1999; www.westingrandvancouver.com*) has a Kids Club® that includes a backpack with crayons, postcards, a Vancouver map and may also include an in-room film voucher and ground level access to loaner pushchairs, high chairs and other useful amenities.

For a list of special treats for kids, check *www.kidsvancouver.com*, which lists year-round and rainy-day things to do such as Granville Island's Public Market, Kids Market shops, water park, street performers, playgrounds and

getting there by Aquabus. Tourism Vancouver has a website section devoted to family and kids' activities (*www.tourismvancouver.com/visitors/ things_to_do/family_and_kids*). Find Family Fun in Vancouver boasts over 250 family activities on its website, *www.findfamilyfun.com*. In addition to museums, parks, aquatic centres and special indoor play areas, the city and neighbouring communities have a host of special events through the year including the Vancouver International Children's Festival (*tel: (604) 708 5655; www.childrensfestival.ca*) in Vanier Park each May. Playland (*Pacific National Exhibition; www.pne.ca*), open from Easter throughout the summer, offers various historic sites and many splashdown parks and water slides. The Cloverdale Rodeo (*tel: (604) 576 9461; www.cloverdalerodeo.com*) in Surrey each Victoria Day is a huge attraction.

Climate

Compared with other cities in Canada, Vancouver and Victoria have a moderate climate, thanks in part to Pacific Ocean currents. There are few extremes in temperature. Vancouver's highest recorded temperature is 33°C (91°F) and the lowest is –18°C (0°F). But clouds and rain can be abundant, especially during the winter months of November, December and January. While about 100cm (39in) of rain falls on Vancouver Airport each year, some areas of the North Shore receive as much as 250cm (98in) annually. As a rule, the summer months of June, July and August are the driest and sunniest. Monthly hours of sunshine average 305 in July and 44 in December. For a recorded weather report, call Environment Canada (*tel: (604) 664 9010*), which also predicts the possibility of rain.

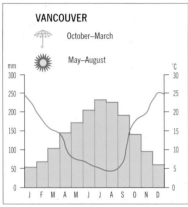

VANCOUVER
October–March
May–August

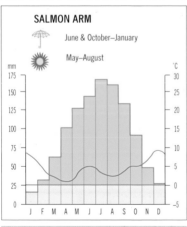

SALMON ARM
June & October–January
May–August

WEATHER CONVERSION CHART

25.4mm = 1 inch

°F = 1.8 × °C + 32

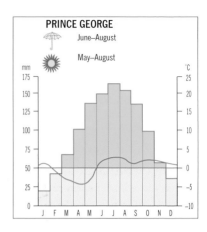

PRINCE GEORGE
June–August
May–August

Consulates

Embassies are located in Ottawa, Canada's capital, but among the consulates in Vancouver are the following:

Australia: *Suite 2050, 1075 West Georgia Street. Tel: (604) 684 1177.*
New Zealand: *888 Dunsmuir Street. Tel: (604) 684 7388.*
UK: *1111 Melville Street. Tel: (604) 683 4421.*
United States: *1075 West Pender Street. Tel: (604) 685 4311.*

Crime

Vancouver is still a generally safe city, compared with such vast urban centres as London and New York. Downtown streets are well lit, but caution and common sense are good watchwords. Report any theft immediately to your hotel and the police.

Customs regulations

Duty-free allowances for visitors aged 19 and older are 200 cigarettes,

50 cigars, 200gm of manufactured tobacco and 200 tobacco sticks; and either 1.5 litres of wine or 1.14 litres of alcohol or a total of 1.14 litres of wine or alcohol or 24 cans or bottles (8.5 litres) of beer or ale, and other dutiable goods up to a limit of $200 in value. There is no duty on personal belongings for use during your visit. Gifts valued at more than $60 are subject to duty and tax on the excess amount. Any currency carried worth $10,000 or more must be declared. Revolvers, pistols and fully automatic firearms are prohibited entry into Canada. Quarantine regulations are strict. Plants must be declared and inspected by Agriculture Canada; animals may be quarantined for up to three months. The Customs website *www.cbsa-asfc.gc.ca* provides full information, but check a short time before you travel because regulations may change frequently.

Driving

Breakdowns

The BC Automobile Association (*tel: (604) 268 5555; www.bcaa.com*) honours memberships of other automobile associations; check with your own association for reciprocity of membership benefits. Automobile club cards are usually valid for discounts at various hotels and attractions. Ask about the Canadian Automobile Association discount when making reservations. For free information on highway conditions, contact Drive BC, the British Columbia government traveller information system

CONVERSION TABLE

FROM	TO	MULTIPLY BY
Inches	Centimetres	2.54
Feet	Metres	0.3048
Yards	Metres	0.9144
Miles	Kilometres	1.6090
Acres	Hectares	0.4047
Gallons	Litres	4.5460
Ounces	Grams	28.35
Pounds	Grams	453.6
Pounds	Kilograms	0.4536
Tons	Tonnes	1.0160

To convert back, for example from centimetres to inches, divide by the number in the third column.

Practical guide

(*freephone: (800) 550 4997; www.drivebc.ca*). The website has links to Highway Cams, weather and ferry information, and similar sites for neighbour provinces. Be prepared for driving on the right side and for variable weather conditions en route. If a breakdown does occur, seek help immediately; stay safe and secure in your car in a well-lit area while awaiting assistance.

Car hire

Hiring a car is relatively inexpensive. Vehicles may be hired through Thomas Cook branches. Major car-hire (rental) companies include:
Alamo (*tel: (604) 683 4537; www.alamo.com*);
Avis (*tel: (604) 606 2869; www.avis.com*);
Budget (*tel: (604) 668 7000; www.budget.com*);
Hertz (*tel: (604) 606 4711; www.hertz.com*).

A major credit card is required to hire a car, even if you plan to pay cash. The Visa Gold Card, among others, provides free car insurance; if you are planning to hire a car for a few weeks, it is worth investing in a gold credit card if you qualify. The minimum age to hire a car is 21, although rental car companies restrict luxury and large vehicle hire to those over the age of 25.

The companies listed above also hire campervans, motorhomes and 4WD vehicles. Chauffeured limousines and other vehicles are also available. Car-hire companies can charge double to fill up the tank, so it is better to do it yourself before returning the car. Remember to drive on the right in Canada, and be sure to check the vehicle operation before leaving the car park.

Petrol

Petrol (gas) is sold by the litre in regular, premium or super grades, all unleaded, and is reasonably priced.

Electricity

Canada's electric current is an alternating 110–120 volts and 60 cycles. Adaptors are sold in hotel shops and at Gulliver's – The Travel Accessory Store at 749 Park Royal North (*tel: (604) 922 9650; www.gulliverstravelstore. com*) and the Sinclair shopping centres.

Emergencies

Ambulance: *911* or *0* for operator.
Dental service: contact your hotel concierge for a recommendation.

Emotional Crisis Centre: *(604) 872 3311; www.crisiscentre.bc.ca*
Fire and rescue: *911* or *0* for operator.
Marine and Aircraft distress: *(800) 567 5111.*
Poison Control Centre: hotline: *(604) 682 5050.*
Police: *911* or *0* for operator.
Prescription Service: contact your hotel concierge; prescriptions are available only by visiting a Canadian doctor.
RCMP Freeway Patrol: *911* or *0* for operator.
Thomas Cook traveller's cheque loss or theft: freephone *00 44 1733 318950* to report lost or stolen cheques within 24 hours (*see also* Money matters, *pp182–3*).

Health

No vaccinations are required for entry into Canada, but a visitor must be healthy upon entry into the country.

Tap water is usually safe to drink. Campers are advised to boil water from lakes and rivers. Canadian healthcare standards are high. If you become ill, ask your hotel to recommend a nearby doctor.

Medical insurance, which should cover the duration of your stay in Canada, is essential as medical services are expensive. A visit to a general practitioner, or a stay in a hospital, could be a costly affair. Carry prescriptions for medication with you – do not pack them – and have your doctor's name and information with you.

Hire facilities

Bicycles

Cycling around Stanley Park and other areas of Vancouver is a wonderful way to explore the city and enjoy the sights. Contact Spokes Bicycle Rentals (*tel: (604) 688 5141; www.vancouverbikerental. com*) at the Georgia Street entrance to the park, or check the Yellow Pages of the telephone directory.

Boats

Sailing boats, motorboats and houseboats are available for hire from dozens of companies both in and outside Vancouver.

Contact the nearest Tourism Visitor Centre for details.

Hitchhiking

Hitchhiking is illegal in British Columbia. For legal and safety reasons, it is not a recommended form of travel.

Insurance

Any medical, baggage or other personal insurance should be purchased before leaving home.

Any vehicle hire automatically includes third-party-liability insurance for damage to people and property. Loss and damage insurance, which covers the hire car, costs extra, as do personal accident insurance and personal effects coverage for the driver and passengers.

Language

Canada has two official languages: English and French. English is the predominant language of BC. First Nations and immigrants from Europe, Asia and around the world speak many other languages, ranging from Chinook to Vietnamese. Canadian English has been most nuanced by Americans, primarily through the media and advertising. Following are a few words that might need some explanation:

Anglophone	English-speaking person
bannock	'Indian' bread
bar	a ridge of sand or gravel in a stream or river where gold may be found by panning, but also a drinking place
First Nations	aboriginal peoples, tribes and bands in Canada
Inuit	Eskimo
Mountie	RCMP officer
potlatch	a First Nations festival with gift-giving
saltchuk	ocean

Lost property

Vancouver has two lost property centres: TransLink (bus, SkyTrain losses) (*Stadium SkyTrain Station, 590 Beatty St; tel: (604) 682 7887; lost.property@ translink.ca*), and the Vancouver Police Department Property Office Lost & Found (*tel: (604) 717 2726*). Otherwise check with the nearest police station or call the head office of BC Transit.

Maps

Maps of Vancouver and BC are available from any Tourism Visitor Centre.

Media

Newspapers and magazines

The best daily in the country, the morning *Globe and Mail* (*www.theglobeandmail.com*), has limited local news. However, *The Province* (*www.theprovince.com*), a tabloid, and *The Vancouver Sun* (*www.vancouversun. com*), a broadsheet, both morning papers, cover city news and events. The *Georgia Straight* (*www.straight.com*) covers the Vancouver arts and entertainment scene. All three are available at newsstands and in street coin boxes. The weekly *Westender* (*www.westender.com*), published on Thursdays, provides compact coverage of entertainment and other downtown and West End events, and is available free at most hotels. The monthly *WHERE Vancouver* (*http://where.ca/vancouver*) is also available in hotels at no charge and for a dollar in coin boxes at the SeaBus Terminal. It is designed especially for visitors and includes information on shopping, dining, attractions, entertainment, special events, maps and evening television programmes.

For general information on what's on in Vancouver, visit *www.showtimetickets. com* (*tel: (604) 688 5000, freephone (800) 480-SHOW*), an online ticket reservation service for concert or theatre events, and Tickets Tonight, which sells half-price tickets for major performances at the Tourism Vancouver Visitor Centre at 200 Burrard Street, plaza level (*tel: (604) 684 2787; www.ticketstonight.ca*).

Radio and television

Favourite local radio stations include CBC at 690 AM, CKNW 980 (talk, music and sport) and QMFM at 103.5 FM (soft rock).

Local television stations include CBC-TV (Canadian Broadcasting Corporation), CTV (the CTV network), and the Knowledge Network (the BC educational channel). Dozens of other channels, including PBS, ABC, CBS and NBC from the USA, are also available locally. Check the listings at the back of *WHERE Vancouver* magazine.

Money matters

Currency

Canada has a decimal currency system with 100 cents to the dollar. Coins are one cent, five cents (a nickel), 10 cents (a dime), 25 cents (a quarter), the one-dollar coin called a 'loonie' (because of the loon bird on one face), and the $2 coin referred to as 'twoonie'. The bills (notes) are colour coded: $5 is blue, $10 is purple, $20 is green, $50 is red and $100 is beige. Merchants seem reluctant to give up a lot of change, so $100 bills are not popular, while $20 bills are always acceptable. Thomas Cook traveller's cheques in Canadian or US dollars are a secure and convenient way of carrying larger amounts of money and can be used as cash in most hotels and restaurants.

Money exchange

Most foreign currencies and traveller's cheques can be exchanged at the foreign exchange counters at Vancouver International Airport, at all major city banks and at some hotels.

Since exchange rates fluctuate, check the Canadian dollar rates on your arrival in Canada. Credit cards, such as American Express, MasterCard and Visa, are widely accepted. ATMs will accept debit cards; however, check the charges before using them as they may be very expensive.

If you need to transfer money quickly, you can use the MoneyGramSM Money transfer service. For more details, *freephone: 0800 897198* (in the UK).

Taxes

British Columbia levies a 12% Harmonised Sales Tax (HST), a single tax that in 2010 incorporated the federal Goods and Service Tax (GST) and the Provincial Sales Tax (PST). BC Children's clothing and food are exempt. Each Canadian province has its own tax system.

National holidays

Banks, post offices, liquor stores, government offices, most other offices and many shops are closed on these holidays. City buses, the SeaBus and the SkyTrain operate on a reduced schedule. Vancouver hotels are rarely fully booked during Canadian holidays, but there are seldom rooms available during American holidays.

New Year's Day 1 January
Good Friday late March, early April
Easter late March, early April
Victoria Day 24 May or the preceding Monday
Canada Day 1 July
BC Day 1 August
Labour Day first Monday in September
Thanksgiving Day second Monday in October
Remembrance Day 11 November
Christmas Day 25 December
Boxing Day 26 December

Opening times

Banks Major banks downtown open at 8am. Some banks are open on Saturday morning, but all are closed on Sundays and holidays. Normal banking hours are 10am–4pm Monday to Friday, often extending to 5pm on Friday.

Museums, galleries and attractions Most are open daily 10am–5pm, but some are closed one day a week, and some have extended or shortened hours on certain days.

Post offices All post offices are open Monday to Friday 8.30am–5.30pm. Some Canada Post sub-offices are open Saturday mornings, and there are postal counters in most 7-Eleven stores.

Shops Most shops and stores are open Monday to Friday 9.30am–6pm, with hours extended to 9pm on Thursday and Friday. Most are open Saturday 9.30am–5.30pm, and many are open on Sunday, noon–5pm. Convenience stores such as 7-Eleven are often open 7am–1am, and some are open all night.

Pharmacies

Medical prescriptions in BC are available only through a local doctor. Many pharmacies are at the back of big drugstores (chemists). These sell all kinds of non-prescription medicines, along with contraceptives, insect repellent, vitamins, tissues and a host of other items. Shoppers Drug Mart, at 1125 Davie Street (*tel: (604) 669 2424*), is open 24 hours a day, seven days a week. London Drugs, at 1187 Robson Street (*tel: (604) 448 4819*), is open from Monday to Saturday 9am–10pm and on Sunday 10am–10pm.

Photography

Many shops sell disposable cameras and supplies for digital cameras. Kerrisdale Cameras, with multiple BC locations, sells equipment and accessories for digital and video cameras, makes prints of digital images, and can help with a malfunctioning camera (*www.kerrisdalecameras.com*).

Copy shops and Internet cafés are good places to burn your photos to CD.

Places of worship

Places of worship representing various denominations and faiths in and around Vancouver include:

Akali Singh Sikh Society Temple
1890 Skeena St. Tel: (604) 254 2117;
http://akalisingh-sikhsociety.ca
Beth Israel Synagogue
4350 Oak St. Tel: (604) 731 4161;
www.bethisraelvan.ca

Canadian Memorial Church
1825 W 16th Ave. Tel: (604) 731 3101;
www.canadianmemorial.org
Central Presbyterian Church
1155 Thurlow St. Tel: (604) 683 1913;
www.centralchurchvancouver.ca
Christ Church Anglican Cathedral
690 Burrard St. Tel: (604) 682 3848;
www.cathedral.vancouver.bc.ca
Christian Science Church
1900 W 12th Ave. Tel: (604) 733 8040;
www.christianscience.bc.ca
First Baptist Church
969 Burrard St. Tel: (604) 683 8441;
www.firstbc.org
Holy Rosary Catholic Cathedral
646 Richards St. Tel: (604) 682 6774;
http://hrc.rcav.org
Ismaili Centre
4010 Canada Way, Burnaby.
Tel: (604) 438 4010; www.theismaili.org

Police

The RCMP (Royal Canadian Mounted Police) cover areas where there is no municipal police force. In an emergency, call *911* or *0* for the operator.

Post offices

The main post office, at 349 West Georgia Street, is open from Monday to Friday 8.30am–5.30pm. Many sub-offices in malls, drugstores, convenience stores and even dry-cleaning shops are open on Saturday as well. Most offer postage, courier and facsimile (fax) services. Canada Post boxes are red. Mail can be received 'c/o General Delivery' at any post office in Canada.

To send a telegram, contact Canada Post.

Senior citizens

Numerous transport and tour companies, hotels, shops, attractions and events offer reduced rates to people as young as 50. Carry an ID card or any other official document that indicates your birth date.

The Hyatt and Westin Bayshore hotels, among others, offer senior discounts. Many local restaurants give 10 to 20 per cent discount to seniors, while others offer small-portion meals and early-bird specials – enquire upon entering any restaurant.

Domestic airlines, the harbour and Granville Island ferries, city transport including the SeaBus and SkyTrain all offer reduced fares to seniors. Call the company directly for details. Such attractions as the Vancouver Aquarium, the Dr Sun Yat-Sen Chinese Garden,

the Vancouver Art Gallery, the Museum of Anthropology, the Maritime Museum, Science World, the Bloedel Floral Conservatory and Grouse Mountain offer reduced admission prices to seniors. The Vancouver Aquatic Centre offers a seniors' programme which includes exercises on the deck and in the pool, and organises day trips outside the city, and such special events as Valentine Tea.

City cinemas, theatres and symphony concerts offer reduced rates to seniors, sometimes by as much as 50 per cent. Some supermarkets, chemists and department stores reduce prices by 10 to 15 per cent one day a month for seniors.

Travel-wise seniors get great holiday bargains through Road Scholar (formerly Elderhostel) (*freephone: (800) 454 5768; www.roadscholar.org*). A monthly publication, the *Independent Times* (*tel: (604) 639 5495; www. theindependenttimes.com*), is geared to

Christ Church Cathedral with the Hotel Vancouver in the background

the needs of 55+-year-old senior readers and can be found at Shoppers Drug Mart or at some banks and visitor centres.

Student and youth travel

Many attractions and events in the Vancouver area offer reduced rates for students. Bring your student card.

Sustainable tourism

Thomas Cook is a strong advocate of ethical and fairly traded tourism and believes that the travel experience should be as good for the places visited as it is for the people who visit them. That's why we firmly support The Travel Foundation, a charity that develops solutions to help improve and protect holiday destinations, their environment, traditions and culture. To find out what you can do to make a positive difference to the places you travel to and the people who live there, please visit *www.thetravelfoundation.org.uk*

Telephones

Although many people use mobile phones, some public telephones can be found in post offices, hotel lobbies, public buildings, and in phone booths on various streets throughout the city. Local calls cost 25 cents to $1 for an unlimited time. Some public phones are specifically for long-distance calls and some are designated for credit card use only. Both local and international calls are usually more expensive on hotel phones. Inexpensive long-distance

phonecards are available under a variety of names and can be purchased at post offices and many other stores. Call *0* for the operator to enquire about discounts for dialling both domestically and abroad at certain times. The area codes for BC are *604* for the Lower Mainland to Hope and north to Whistler, and *250* for the rest of the province; some numbers with the area code *778* were allotted when *250* and *604* were fully subscribed.

International calls can be dialled direct using the following codes: Britain is *011* + *44* + city code minus the initial *0* + number, Australia *011* + *61* + city code + number, and New Zealand *011* + *64* + city code + number. For calls to other provinces of Canada and to the USA, dial 1, the area code and the number.

Ticket agencies

For such events as opera, symphony concerts, ballet, theatre, sports, rock concerts and some attractions, call Ticketmaster on *(604) 280 4444; www.ticketmaster.ca*, with box office locations in downtown Vancouver (*Tourism Vancouver, 200 Burrard St; General Motors Place, 800 Griffiths Way; and Van City Sports, 554 West Georgia St*). Ticketmaster has special lines for arts events (*tel: (604) 280 3311*) and spectator sports (*tel: (604) 280 4400*). Cinema tickets are sold only at individual theatres.

Time

Most of BC is on Pacific Standard Time, which in summer is seven hours behind GMT. Clocks are put back an hour on the first Sunday in November, and an hour forward on the second Sunday in March, for daylight-saving time. Vancouver time is the same as California, and three hours behind Toronto and New York. For most of the year, Vancouver is 18 hours behind Sydney and 21 hours behind Auckland.

Tipping

Tips generally range from 10 to 20 per cent in restaurants and bars, and for taxis. Tipping is optional for porters, doormen, chambermaids and other service personnel.

Toilets

Public toilets are found in railway and bus terminals, shopping centres and department stores. A hotel or restaurant will sometimes let you use its facilities.

Tourist offices

For maps and brochures on Vancouver and BC, contact Tourism British Columbia (*tel: (604) HelloBC, freephone (800) HelloBC; www.hellobc.com*). The website has a complete list of visitor (information) centres.

Tours

UK-based travellers can pre-book a range of tours and travel options at advantageous rates when arranging their trip with Thomas Cook Holidays (details from any branch of Thomas Cook, or if in the UK by telephoning

01733 417000). Visitors to Vancouver can take to the water aboard the SeaBus or the Aquabus to Granville Island and BC ferries, in a canoe or kayak, or on a motorboat or yacht. Landlubbers can tour on foot and by bicycle, antique car, bus, train or limousine. Some visitors take to the air in seaplanes, gliders, helicopters and hot-air balloons. Although North American travellers tend to be do-it-yourself sightseers or rely on friends and relatives, numerous commercial tours are available, especially in summer. Many can be pre-booked within your overall travel plan. The *Official Visitors' Guide* booklet, stocked at visitor centres, is helpful (and can also be requested through *www.tourismvancouver.com* or *www.hellobc.com*).

Bicycle tours

The Vancouver Bicycle Club (*tel: (604) 733 3964; http://vbc.bc.ca*) welcomes non-members to join in city cycling and tours further afield.

Bus and car tours

Gray Line (*freephone: (800) 667 0882; www.graylinewest.com*) for Victoria and Pacific Coach Lines in Vancouver (*freephone (800) 661 1725; www.pacificcoach.com*) offers various sightseeing tours, with itineraries ranging from a city circle, similar to the Trolley tour routes (*see pp36–7*), and an evening dinner tour (a great way to meet fellow travellers), to a seven-day return ride through the Rockies to Calgary. In Victoria, Gray Line West uses a 1926 Ford Model T or classic convertible cars from the 1950s and 1960s for four-hour Ride-n-Style Classic Car Tours. LimoJet Gold (*tel: (604) 273 1331, freephone (800) 278 8742; www.limojetgold.com*) creates tailored tours in the luxury of a limousine, day or night, in addition to airport and intercity transfer.

Historic walking tours

Local historian John Atkin (*www.johnatkin.com*), who probably knows Vancouver past and present better than anyone, offers walking tours of the city centre and neighbourhoods. The Vancouver Historical Society (*tel: (604) 878 9140; www.vancouver-historical-society.ca*) offers occasional walking tours – call for the schedule.

Water tours

In Victoria, Gray Line (*tel: (800) 667 0882; www.graylinewest.com*) and the SS *Beaver* paddle wheeler (*tel: (250) 294 3950; www.ssbeaver.ca*) offer harbour sightseeing excursions. Harbour Cruises offers a four-hour lunch tour to Indian Arm (*tel: (604) 688 7246; www.boatcruises.com*).

Sewell's Marina (*tel: (604) 921 3474; www.sewellsmarina.com*) in Horseshoe Bay offers skippered fishing and other tours. For white-water rafting from May to September, contact Hyak Wilderness Adventures (*tel: (800) 663 7238; www.hyak.com*).

Transport
Airlines
Air Canada (*tel: (888) 247 2262; www.aircanada.com*)
Harbour Air (*tel: (604) 274 1277, freephone (800) 665 0212; www.harbour-air.com*)
Helijet Airways (*freephone: (800) 665 4354; www.helijet.com*)
West Jet Airlines (*freephone: (888) 937 8538; www.westjet.com*)

Buses
Gray Line (*tel: (800) 667 0882; www.graylinewest.com*) offers Victoria sightseeing tours.
Greyhound (*tel: (800) 661 8747; www.greyhound.ca*) operates throughout Canada.
Pacific Coach Lines (*tel: (800) 661 1725; www.pacificcoach.com*) YVR Whistler SkyLynx connects Vancouver International Airport to Whistler, and offers sightseeing trips between Vancouver and Victoria.
TransLink (*tel: (604) 953 3333; www.translink.ca*), Vancouver's regional public transport system, includes buses, the SeaBus and the SkyTrain, which run along major arteries through the city centre and suburbs. There are three fare zones in Greater Vancouver. Day passes are available for children and senior citizens. Exact change in coins is preferred, but tickets and passes are sold at 7-Eleven and other stores.

Transit timetables are available from public libraries, city and municipal

halls, Tourism Visitor Centres and
TransLink offices and terminals. For
Blue Bus routes and schedules from
downtown to West Vancouver, call
(604) 985 7777; http://westvancouver.ca

The SeaBuses, which are actually
400-passenger catamaran ferries, make
the 15-minute trip across Burrard Inlet
to North Vancouver every 15 minutes.
The SkyTrain (*www.translink.ca*) runs
from downtown Vancouver to
Burnaby, Westminster and Surrey,
while the SkyTrain Canada Line runs
from Vancouver International Airport
to downtown.

Ferries
The little Aquabus ferries (*www.
theaquabus.com*) operating from the
foot of Hornby Street, and the False
Creek Ferries (*www.granvilleislandferries.
bc.ca*) from the Aquatic Centre, make
the run to and from Granville Island all
year round. BC Ferries (*tel: (888) 223
3779; www.bcferries.ca*) carry both
vehicles and foot passengers and run
from Tsawwassen (an hour's drive
south from the city centre) to Swartz
Bay (a half-hour from Victoria) and
Nanaimo on Vancouver Island, and to
the Gulf Islands. From Horseshoe Bay
(a half-hour drive northwest from
downtown Vancouver), ferries sail to
Nanaimo, Bowen Island and the
Sunshine Coast.

Taxis
It is hard to hail a taxi in downtown
Vancouver – the best approach is

probably to head to the nearest big
hotel, where taxis usually wait in line,
or call a cab; here are some choices:
Black Top & Checker Cabs
(*tel: (604) 731 1111;
http://blacktopcheckercabs.supersites.ca*).
Yellow Cab
(*tel: (604) 681 1111;
www.yellowcabonline.com*).

Trains
VIA Rail (*tel: (888) 842 7245; www.
viarail.ca*) operates a thrice-weekly
passenger service across Canada,
departing from the station on Main
Street opposite Science World. VIA
Rail's Canadian train runs from
Toronto to Vancouver and can be
booked outside Canada. So can **Rocky
Mountaineer** (*www.rockymountaineer.
com*) trips, which go from Vancouver to
Whistler, or to Jasper, to Banff and on
to Calgary (*see p136*).

Details of local rail, bus and ferry
services are shown in the Thomas
Cook Overseas Timetable, which is
available to buy online from
www.thomascookpublishing.com, from
Thomas Cook branches in the UK or
by phoning *01733 416477*.

Travellers with disabilities
For information on facilities for
people with disabilities, contact any
Tourism Visitor Centre, or the BC
Paraplegic Association, at 780
Southwest Marine Drive, BC V6P 5Y7
(*tel: (604) 324 3611;
www.canparaplegic.org*).

Index

A
accommodation 113, 132–3, 172–5, 176–7
Active Pass Lighthouse 101
aerial sightseeing 24
air travel 8, 103, 176, 188
Ambleside Beach 27
angling 116, 125, 160–61
aquarium 66–7, 154
Atlin Lake 128

B
ballet 149
Banff National Park 138
banks 183
Bastion, The 111
BC Farm Museum 85
BC Golf Museum and Hall of Fame 53
BC Museum of Mining 83
BC Sports Hall of Fame and Museum 53
beaches 25–7, 69, 99, 105, 112–13, 114, 122, 127
bears 66, 86
beavers 64
birds 63–4, 73, 103, 105, 108–9, 113, 114, 130
Blackcomb 83, 158
boats and ships 8, 12, 54, 65, 68, 74–5, 88–9, 96, 100, 103, 117–19, 122, 126–7, 128–32, 160, 161, 181, 188–9
Bowen Island 96–7
bowling 156
Bowron Lakes 128
Brighton Park 70
Brockton Point 68
Broken Islands 119
Buddhist Temple 59
bungee and ropes courses 156
buses 187–9
Butchart Gardens 106–7
Butterfly World & Gardens 115

C
camping 132, 173, 176–7
Canada Place Pier 22, 24, 40, 65
Canadian Memorial Church 59–60
Canadian Museum of Flight 53
canoeing 128, 130–31, 160
Capilano River 80
Capilano Salmon Hatchery 76, 80
Capilano Suspension Bridge 80, 155
car hire 179–80, 181

Cariboo Chilcotin 18, 126
Carr, Emily 42–3
Cartwright Street 57
Cates Park 82
Cathedral Grove 114
caving 156
Century's Winds of Change Mural 30
Chemainus 110
children 53–4, 61–2, 66–7, 107, 112–13, 154–5, 177
Children's Farmyard 66
Chilko River 130
Chinese Canada 20, 28, 30–33, 164–5
Chinese Cultural Centre 28, 30
Christ Church Anglican Cathedral 60
churches 59–60, 101, 184
cinema 55, 148, 150–51
climate 8, 9, 16, 18, 26, 27, 39, 118, 126–7, 177–8
climbing 83, 157
Coal Harbour 72
Comox 125
concessions 177, 179, 185, 186
consulates 178
conversion table 179
Coombs 114–15
Courtenay and District Museum 125
Courtyard, The 35
Craig Heritage Park and Museum 113
credit cards 180
Creston Valley 130–31
crime 178
culture and events 14–15, 40–43 see also individual terms
Cultus Lake 76–7
currency 110, 182–3
customs and duty 178–9
cycling 68–9, 156, 181, 187
Cypress Provincial Park 78, 81–2, 157, 158

D
Deighton, 'Gassy' Jack 35
Delkatla Wildlife Sanctuary 103, 105
Della Falls 133
Desolation Sound 128
disabilities 189
discos and clubs 151–2
Dr Sun Yat-Sen Chinese Garden 28, 30–31
dress 16, 118
driving 16–17, 124–5, 179–80, 181, 188
Duranleau Street 56

E
earthquakes 7
electricity 180
emergencies 180
Emily Carr University of Art + Design 57
English Bay 25, 26
Englishman River Falls Provincial Park 115
entry formalities 176
environmental issues 8, 43, 61, 63, 120–21, 186
ethnicity 4–5, 9, 20, 28, 29, 30–33, 35, 164–7 see also First Nations
etiquette and mores 16, 17–18, 118

F
False Creek 73
ferries 74–5, 96, 100, 103, 117–19, 188–9
Ferry Building 98
First Nations 29, 34, 38, 42–3, 49–53, 69, 80, 102–3, 105, 107, 110–11, 124, 138, 140, 141
flora and fauna 86–7, 94–5 see also individual entries
food and drink 18, 27, 31, 35, 45, 56, 57, 74, 110, 111, 113, 115, 122, 151, 164–71
forests 8, 46–7, 63, 80, 82, 114, 117, 120–21
Fort Langley 85
Fort Langley National Historic Site 85, 88
Fort Steele 139
Fraser, Simon 130
Fraser River 10, 88–9, 130, 131
fruit picking 76

G
Galiano Island 100
galleries 29, 34, 38, 43, 110, 114, 140–41, 183
gambling 150
Gaoler's Mews 35
garage sales 76
gardens 28, 30–31, 39, 44, 90–91, 106–7, 114
Garry Point Park 93
Gastown 20, 29, 34–5
geese 113
geography 6–8
Gertrude Lawson House 98–9
Gibsons 124
gold mining 139

golf 53, 113, 114, 156–7
gondola rides 78
Granville Island 20, 38, 56–7, 148, 154–5
Greater Vancouver Zoo 66
Grouse Mountain 78, 80, 157, 158
Gulf Islands 100–102, 129
Gulf of Georgia Cannery National Historic Site 93
Gwaii Haanas National Park Reserve 102–3

H
H R MacMillan Space Centre 53–4, 154
Haida Gwaii 102–3, 105
Haida Heritage Centre 105
Harbour View Park 70
Harrison Hot Springs 89–91
Harrison Lake 89
health 180, 184
Helmcken House 107
history 4, 6–7, 10–12, 32–3, 50–51, 85, 100–101, 134
hitchhiking 181
horse racing 162
horse riding 126, 136–7, 157
Hudson's Bay Company 85
Hunlen Lakes 133

I
Indian Arm 82
insurance 180, 181
Irving House 45

J
Jasper National Park 138–9
jazz 152

K
kayaking 161
Keefer Street 31
Kerrisdale 20
Kimberley 139
Kitsilano 20
Kitsilano Beach 25
Kootenay National Park 139

L
Landing, The 34
Langley Centennial Museum 85
language 181
Le Gavroche 45, 166–7
Lighthouse Park 99
Little Qualicum Falls Provincial Park 115

logging and lumber 27, 116, 120–21
Long Beach 122
Lonsdale Quay 74–5
Lost Lagoon 64
lost property 181
Lumberman's Arch 68

M
magazines 148, 182
Manning Provincial Park 137
map outlets 181, 187
Maple Tree Square 35
Marine Building 40
markets 56, 77, 144–6
Mayne Island 100–102
Mayne Island Gaol 101
Minter Gardens 90–91
money 110, 180, 182–3
Monument of Canadian Chinese 31
Moresby Island 103
Mount Arrowsmith 116
Mount Edziza Provincial Park 137
Mount Robson Provincial Park 132
Mount Seymour Provincial Park 78, 82, 157, 158
murals 30, 110
Museum of Anthropology 49, 52–3, 155
Museum of Vancouver 54
museums 49, 52–4, 83, 85, 93, 98–9, 101, 107, 111, 113, 125, 154, 155, 183
music 14–15, 55, 114, 148, 149, 151–3

N
Naikoon Provincial Park 105
Nanaimo 111
Nanaimo Museum 111
national holidays 183
newspapers 148, 182, 185–6
Nine O'Clock Gun 68
Nitobe Memorial Garden 39
northern British Columbia 18–19
Nuyumbalees Cultural Centre 105

O
Okanagan Lake 129
Okanagan Valley 126
Old School House, The 114
opening times 183
opera 149
Orpheum 55, 58, 149

P
Pacific Rim National Park Reserve 122–3
Pacific Spirit Regional Park 46–7
packing 16, 118
paragliding 157
Park and Tilford Gardens 39
parks 9, 18, 39, 40–41, 99, 132 see also individual entries
Parksville 112–13
Parksville Beach 112
Parliament Buildings 107
Peace Arch Park 91–3
Pender Islands 102
Pender Street 31
Petroglyph Provincial Park 110–11
pharmacies 184
photography 184
places of worship 59–60, 101, 184
Point Atkinson Lighthouse 99
police 184
politics 13
Port Alberni 116–17
Portside Park 65, 70
post 183, 184–5
Powell River 125
Princess Louisa Inlet 129
Prospect Point 69
Purcell Mountains 126

Q
Quadra Island 105–6
Qualicum Beach 114
Queen Elizabeth Park 39, 44

R
raccoons 87
radio 182
rafting 130, 131–2, 161
Rathtrevor Beach Provincial Park 112–13
Reid, Bill 52
Reifel Bird Sanctuary 109
revolving viewpoints 24–5
Richmond 20
Robertson Creek Hatchery 117
Robson Street 20, 140
rock and pop 152–3
Rockies 8, 18, 126, 136, 138–9
Roedde House 45, 48
rowing 68
Royal BC Museum 107

S
safety 17, 27, 130, 178, 179, 180
St Mary Magdalene's 101

salmon 76, 80, 93, 96–7, 111, 116, 117, 160
Salt Spring Island 102
Sam Kee Building 30
Saturna Island 102
Savary Island 127
Science World 61–2, 154
scuba diving 161–2
Sea to Sky Highway 83
Sea Village 57
seasons 9, 16, 26, 39, 126–7, 177–8
Sechelt 124
Second Beach 25, 69
senior citizens 185–6
Shannon Falls Provincial Park 83
Shaughnessy 20, 48
shopping 31, 34, 56, 71, 74–5, 140–47, 183
Shuswap Lake 129
Sicamous 129
skiing 81, 83, 157–60
Skookumchuk Narrows Provincial Park 124–5
smoking 17
snorkelling 111
sport and leisure 156–63 see also individual entries
springs 8, 89
Sproat Lake 116–17
Squamish 83
Stamp River Provincial Park 117
Stanley Park 37, 63–4, 65, 66–9, 87, 154
Stawamus Chief 83
Steam Clock 34–5
Steveston 93
Steveston Museum 93
Strathcona Provincial Park 132–3
student travel 186
Sunset Beach 25, 27
Sunshine Coast 124
Surrey 20
sustainable tourism 186
swimming 162

T
Tatlayoko Lake 137
taxes 183
taxis 189
telephones 186
television 182
tennis 160
theatre 55, 58, 150, 153
Third Beach 25
Thompson Okanagan 19
Thunderbird Park 107
tickets 148, 182, 186
time differences 186–7
tipping 187
Tofino 122
toilets 187

totem poles 49, 51, 52, 103, 107
tourist information 181, 187
tours 36–7, 48, 74–5, 124–5, 187–8
trains 11, 66, 134–6, 188–9
traveller's cheques 180, 182–3
trolleys 36–7
Tweedsmuir Provincial Park 133
Two Sisters 80

U
Ucluelet 122
University of British Columbia Botanical Garden 44

V
Vancouver, George 53
Vancouver Aquarium 66–7, 154
Vancouver Chinatown Millennium Gate 30
Vancouver Harbour 65, 70, 72–3
Vancouver Island 19, 106–7, 110–19, 122–3, 126
Vancouver Maritime Museum 54
Vancouver Rowing Club 68
Vancouver Symphony Orchestra 55
VanDusen Botanical Garden 44
Victoria 5, 106–7
volcanoes 7

W
walks 30–31, 34–5, 40–41, 46–7, 48, 56–7, 81, 82, 89–90, 96–7, 99, 117, 122–3, 157, 188
waterfalls 83, 115, 117, 133
Waterfront Park 70, 75
Wells Gray Provincial Park 133
West Coast Trail 122–3
West Vancouver 20, 98
Westminster Abbey 60
whales 67, 122, 163
Whistler 83
Whistler resort 82–4, 158
Wing Sang Building 31
Wreck Beach 25

Y
Yaletown 20, 70–71, 73
Yoho National Park 139
youth travel 186

Z
zoos 66

Acknowledgements

Thomas Cook Publishing wishes to thank HELENA ZUKOWSKI to whom the copyright belongs, for the photographs in this book, except for the following images:

PICTURES COLOUR LIBRARY 1, 16, 17, 24, 43, 62, 70, 71, 72, 101, 110, 116, 145, 159, 169
PAM MANDEL 18, 87, 165
WORLD PICTURES/PHOTOSHOT 26, 73, 118, 123, 135, 141, 166
DREAMSTIME 28 (Natalia Bratslavsky)
KAREN BEAULAH 44
ROY STEWART 48, 81
MUSEUM OF ANTHROPOLOGY/BILL MCLENNAN 42, 52
CHIEN-HSIN KUO/VANCOUVER CIVIC THEATRES 58
MILLIE WAN/INTERNATIONAL BUDDHIST SOCIETY 59
VANCOUVER AQUARIUM/DIANE MORRISON 66
JULIE CRANE 77
GROUSE MOUNTAIN RESORT 80
WIKIMEDIA COMMONS 83 (Jeff Yang); 84, 185 (Thomas Quine); 117 (Clayoquot); 146, 147, 151 (Arnold C); 171 (Kingnothing83)
RICHARD SHAPKA 99, 108
LADY ROSE MARINE SERVICES 119
CHRIS POTTER 121
DAVID BLUE/BARD ON THE BEACH 149
JEFF VINNICK/VANCOUVER CANUCKS 163

For CAMBRIDGE PUBLISHING MANAGEMENT LTD:
Project editor: Penny Isaac
Typesetter: Paul Queripel
Proofreaders: Karolin Thomas & Lucilla Watson
Indexer: Karolin Thomas

SEND YOUR THOUGHTS TO
BOOKS@THOMASCOOK.COM

We're committed to providing the very best up-to-date information in our travel guides and constantly strive to make them as useful as they can be. You can help us to improve future editions by letting us have your feedback. If you've made a wonderful discovery on your travels that we don't already feature, if you'd like to inform us about recent changes to anything that we do include, or if you simply want to let us know your thoughts about this guidebook and how we can make it even better – we'd love to hear from you.

Send us ideas, discoveries and recommendations today and then look out for your valuable input in the next edition of this title.

Emails to the above address, or letters to the traveller guides Series Editor, Thomas Cook Publishing, PO Box 227, Coningsby Road, Peterborough PE3 8SB, UK.

Please don't forget to let us know which title your feedback refers to!